Discovering

𝕮𝖑𝖆𝖘𝖘𝖎𝖈

Horror

Fiction I

Edited by
Darrell
Schweitzer

WILDSIDE PRESS
P.O. Box 45
Gillette, NJ 07933-0045

WILDSIDE PRESS
P.O. Box 45
Gillette, NJ 07933-0045

Contents

Introduction

"The oldest and strongest emotion of mankind is fear," writes H. P. Lovecraft in "Supernatural Horror in Literature," and while the *fantastic* may be the oldest mode of storytelling, dating back to *The Epic of Gilgamesh* and to Homer, the actual literature of fear is of more recent invention. Perhaps it takes a more sophisticated, rationalistic culture to enjoy stories deliberately designed to scare the reader, or more seriously, to explore the nature of our fears. There are frightening parts in medieval romance, in traditional balladry, and in sagas and epics, but the primary thrust of those works is elsewhere. There might have been a flourishing horror literature in the earlier centuries of the Roman Empire, when educated men inclined toward skepticism. The werewolf episode in *The Satyricon* and the riot of (frequently terrifying) supernaturalism in *The Golden Ass* of Apuleius suggest a large body of such fiction, since these two highly-developed works could not have been written in isolation, but not enough has survived to tell.

Perhaps it is that when people truly fear the supernatural they are unwilling to play games with it in literature, much less use supernatural-dread to symbolize something else, as Henry James, Walter de la Mare, Lovecraft, and so many others have done. So, the supernatural horror story, as distinct from other forms of fantasy, has developed relatively recently.

The classic period in English-language supernatural horror extends roughly from 1833 (the first Poe stores) to 1937 (the death of Lovecraft). Earlier, Gothics flourished, *The Castle of Otranto, The Monk, Melmoth the Wanderer* and the whole chain-rattling crew. Afterwards, the modern horror tale developed and is still developing. The distinction between classic and modern is not yet clear. We can only say that post-Lovecraftian horror fiction "feels" different. David Hartwell has suggested that with L. Ron Hubbard's *Fear* (1940) and Fritz Leiber's *Conjure Wife* (1943) the horror story turned distinctly inward, so that the state of the protagonist's mind became fully as important as any external menace. But these observations are never hard and fast. "The Turn of the Screw" or "Seaton's Aunt" are surely as involved with the mind as with externally existing spooks, and many Stephen King stories are quite unambiguous

. about the objective reality of their menaces. Whole books will doubtless be written on this topic.

The present volume is the first in a series dealing with horror writers of the classic period. As my *Discovering Modern Horror Fiction* might be called a book of Stephen King criticism, only about everybody else, so this one is *Discovering H.P. Lovecraft* — only about everybody else. It is too easy to forget that the few giants exist in a larger context. Our contributors now attempt to supply some of that context. The whole purpose of this series is to supply secondary material on significant writers in greater depth than encyclopedia entries, but in a format more affordable than such massive works as E.F. Bleiler's (admittedly superb, but prohibitively expensive) *Supernatural Fiction Writers*.

Of course dozens of worthy writers have been left out due to space limitations. That's what future volumes are for.

Happy Hauntings.

— Darrell Schweitzer
September 1991

vi

Arthur Machen:
Philosphy and Fiction
S. T. Joshi

Arthur Machen's place in horror literature is secure. Along with Algernon Blackwood and M. R. James, Machen (1863-1947) was the leading figure in what Philip Van Doren Stern aptly termed the "golden age" of the horror story, spanning roughly the period 1880-1920. His landmark works of the 1890s—"The Great God Pan," "The White People," *The Three Imposters* (containing "The Novel of the Black Seal:" and "The Novel of the White Powder"), *The Hill of Dreams*—are not only too well known to require citation, but in no small way contributed to the atmosphere of sophisticated diabolic that distinguishes the "Yellow Nineties."

Machen's influence in the field has been similarly widespread. He was almost idolised by H. P. Lovecraft, who not only ranked "The White People" along with Blackwood's "The Willows" as the two finest horror tales ever written (a judgment that may not be far from wrong), but referred to him by name in his own fiction, notably in the very Machenian "The Whisperer in Darkness." Machen's short novel T*he Terror* is, one supposes, the prototype of the "animals revolt against man" theme, and can therefore be reckoned an influence upon such later works as Daphne du Maurier's "The Birds" and Philip MacDonald's wicked short story "Our Feathered Friends." More recently, T. E. D. Klein has transparently acknowledged the Machen influence in his novel *The Ceremonies* (1984), which is Machenian not only in texture but even in conception.

But Machen was far more than a horror writer. Indeed, even if we consider the bulk of his fiction to be horrific (and, as we shall see, there may be reason to doubt even this), there is certainly nothing of horror in the picaresque *The Chronicle of Clemendy*. What is more, Machen's nonfictional writing dwarfs his fiction many times over. Some of this material is tangentially related to his horror writing—many have, perhaps, believed that *The Canning Wonder* is a novel, but it is in fact a prosy historical work about an odd disappearance in the eighteenth century—but much is not. His voluminous essays cover the most diverse subjects—literature, religion, history, occultism, philosophy—and he wrote a staggering quantity of newspaper articles (especially when he was a reporter

1

for The *The London Evening News)* and book reviews. Machen's translation of Casanova's *Memoirs* is still standard, and he was also the author of autobiographies, religious tracts, and many prefaces and introductions to other authors' books.

Given this diversity of output, is there any chance that there could be some unity to this chaos? How are we to reconcile Machen the author of the sensitive *bildungsroman, The Hill of Dreams,* and Machen the author of the vicious polemic against Protestantism, *Dr. Stiggins?* Curiously, this reconciliation is surprisingly easy, for the more we read Machen, the more we see that nearly the whole of his output is inspired by one idea, and one only: the awesome and utterly unfathomable mystery of the universe.

The matter is made clear in his pamphlet *Beneath the Barley* (1931), where he described the origin of his juvenile poem *Eleusinia:*

> For literature, as I see it, is the art of describing the indescribable; the art of exhibiting symbols which may hint at the ineffable mysteries behind them; the art of the veil, which reveals what it conceals.

Similarly, his *Hieroglyphics: A Note upon Ecstasy in Literature* (1902) is, for all its questionable merits as a handbook of aesthetic theory, a transparent elucidation of his own literary goals. to be called literature (as opposed to what Machen contemptuously called "reading matter"), a word must contain *ecstasy.* What is ecstasy? Machen admits that the term is too nebulous to define, but provides representative synonyms:

> Substitute, if you like, rapture, beauty, adoration, wonder, awe, mystery, sense of the unknown, desire for the unknown . . . In every case there will be that withdrawal from the common life and the common consciousness which justifies my choice of "ecstasy": as the best symbol of my meaning.[1]

A later quotation may in fact provide us with all the background we need to understand Machen's work:

> Man is a sacrament, soul manifested under the form of body, and art has to deal with each and both and to show their interaction and interdependence.[2]

2

The notions of ecstasy, of the veil, and of the sacrament: can these be sufficient to unlock the mysteries of Machen's entire output? I rather think so, since in spite of the superficial variety of form and genre, Machen's work returns again and again to these basic principles; so often, indeed—especially in his staggering quantity of articles and journalism—that the analysis of a few works will explicate them all.

I have no intention of examining Machen's philosophy—if it can be called that—in any greater detail, save to note that the embracing of the above tenets involved Machen in as systematic a rearguard opposition to the course of modern civilization as it is possible to imagine. It is in fact much easier to tell what Machen hates and despises than what he loves and worships; Wesley Sweetser has made a succinct list:

> To him, the enemies of the spirit were big business, industrialization, science, naturalism, democracy, Puritanism, Protestantism, atheism, and Communism. [3]

Some of these—business and industrialism—are easy targets, and it is hard to find any significant writer of the time defending them; others—religious issues—are purely matters of upbringing and temperament, although the depth and sincerity of Machen's Roman Catholicism can scarcely be doubted. It is precisely the fervency of his beliefs that inspired the ferocious satire of *Dr. Stiggins* (1906), where a Protestant minister condemns himself out of his own mouth, and such a work as *War and the Christian Faith* (1918), where Machen tries to refute atheism (on the fatuous and irrelevant claim that it leads to despair) and to bolster the belief— whcih many at that time quite understandably found difficult to accept—in the omnipotence and benevolence of God.

The battle against science and materialism is one that Machen never relinquished, for he regarded these two foes as the most ominous evils of the day. But Machen's attacks on them are strangely feeble and off the mark. To Machen, science deals only with the surfaces of things—the body, as it were, not the soul. As he very prettily puts it in *The Secret Glory*,

> Our great loss is that we separate what is one and make it two; and then, having done so, we make the less real into the more real, as if we thought the glass made to hold wine more important than the wine it holds. [4]

It is an interesting analogy, but a false one, since Machen has never established that the soul actually exists. In any case, most of Machen's polemics end up attacking a ridiculously caricatured version of science and rationalism, as in the following astonishing passage from *Hieroglyphics*:

1. Explain, in rational terms, *The Quest of the Holy Graal*. State whether in your opinion such a vessel ever existed, and if you think it did not, justify your pleasure in reading the account of the search for it.
2. Explain, logically, your delight in colour. State, in terms that Voltaire would have understood, the meaning of that phrase, "the beauty of line."
3. What do you mean by the word "music"? Give the rational explanations of Bach's Fugues, showing them to be as (1) true as Biology and (2) useful as Applied Mechanics.
4. Estimate the value of Westminster Abbey in the avoirdupois measure.
5. "The light that never was on land or sea." What light?
6. "Faery lands forlorn." Draw a map of the district in question, putting in principal towns and naming exports.
7. Show that "heaven lies about us in our infancy" must mean "wholesome maternal influences surround us in our childhood."[5]

Or see how the wonderful richness of Frazer's anthropological speculations in *The Golden Bough* is travestied in the following:

Of course, I am quite willing to allow that, as a general rule, an anxiety about the spring crops fully explains the origin of all painting, all sculpture, all architecture, all poetry, all drama, all music, all religion, all romance: I admit that the Holy Gospels are really all about spring cabbage, that Arthur is really arator, the ploughman; that Galahad, denoting the achievement and end of the great quest, is Caulahad, the cabbage god. I admit all this because it is so entirely reasonable and satisfactory, and, indeed, self-evident; but though all Frazerdom should rise

4

against me, I cannot allow that when I lit my dark lantern
I was inviting the sun to help the crops.[6]

When I read passages like this I want to look for the nearest
wall to bang my head against. It is not merely that Machen has not
understood the views he is attacking; it is that he has made no attempt to do so. No self-respecting scientist would ascribe to the
moronic reductionism Machen attributes to his opponents. Machen
also finds science irritating for requiring reasoned explanations for
everything: since everything is ultimately a mystery (something
which, interestingly enough, Machen's contemporary Ludwig
Wittgenstein would have had no trouble accepting, although from
an entirely different perspective), why bother with explanations? In
the story "Out of the Picture" he says it is as unreasonable for a
medium to give an account of her gift of prophecy as it is for a poet
to give an account of his genius. [7] But whereas the medium is
putting forth claims to *literal* truth, the poet is only expressing
aesthetic truths. Machen makes this sort of category mistake time
and again.

Machen's opposition to liberalism and democracy can be seen
as another sign of his traditionalism; but I believe there is a more
dangerous side to it. He is endlessly fond of abusing Macaulay for
the latter's criticism that Plato's philosophy led to no practical benefit for mankind whereas Bacon's did; and in "Out of the Picture"
he declares: "There is something eminently human in the desire
of impossible things. To seek for possibilities is rather the business
of the lower animals than of man." [8] Machen invites us to interpret this statement politically and socially, and, far from a harmless
aestheticism, the implication is nothing less than fascism. It is very
well for Machen, in the comfort of his civil list pension, to ponder
the mysteries of the universe, but this is not much consolation for
the homeless man. It is all the more remarkable that Machen would
be led to this thoughtless attitude in light of the grinding poverty
that dogged much of his own life.

Machen's remarks on literary realism are somewhat more interesting. It could be expected of one who could not bear to read
Conrad[9] that he would oppose realism: "The Artist with a capital
A is not a clever photographer who understands selection in a
greater or less degree." [10] This is because what we call the "real
world" is not in fact real: "We live in a world of symbols; of sensible perishable thing which both veil and reveal spiritual and liv-

5

ing and eternal realities." [11] The only true "realism", therefore, is symbolism, because the symbol *is* the reality, or at least as close to the ineffable reality as we can get.

The sole goal of Machen's philosophy is to restore the sense of wonder and mystery into our perception of the world; everything that tended to foster such a goal—mysticism, occultism, Catholicism, symbolism—were to be encouraged, and everything that hindered it—Protestantism (criticised as appealing too much to the rational intellect), science, rationalism, realism—were to be furiously combated. But Machen was no philosopher; the telling sign of this is the fact that his views never changed through the whole course of his long life. Unlike his admirer H. P. Lovecraft, who progressed from doctrinaire materialism to a reasoned understanding of the uncertainties of modern astrophysics, from radical political conservatism to moderate socialism, from a naive and affected archaism of style and manner to a spare yet powerful modernism of tone, Machen's monolithic views remained unaffected by any new insights. He embraced not so much a philosophy as a series of prejudices which he guarded with a dogged tenacity against opposing views he could not understand or approach sympathetically.

So much for Machen's philosophy; what of his fiction? Here we will find another remarkable circumstance: although he wrote novels and stories from the age of twenty to the age of sixty, nearly all his best work was produced within the single decade of 1889-1899—not coincidental, the one period in his life when, thanks to a timely inheritance, he did not have to support himself and could devote all his energies to writing. The chronology of Machen's stories does not at all correspond to their dates of publication, and it is worth while to have some idea of the sequence of his fiction-writing (see Appendix).

What strikes us about Machen is the number of works that can be totally dispensed with or ignored without affecting our understanding of him. Indeed, it might have been better if Machen had done a similar purging. Machen's worst flaw—over and above his insubstantial philosophy, his clumsy polemics, his total lack of narrative skill—is that he wrote too much. We have already noticed this in his nonfictional writing: *Dr. Stiggins* was not read in his day and is unreadable in ours; *The Canning Wonder* (1926) is a mind-numbingly tedious account of a strange disappearance in the eighteenth century—an account he had previously written up in at least two shorter versions; [12] and his very first work (excluding, of course, *Eleusinia* (1881), a rather able poem for a seventeen-year-old), *The Anatomy of Tobacco* (1884), is an intolerably precious attempt to mingle scholastic philosophy with Machen's fondness for tobacco. No one need criticise Machen for *writing* this work—it is the sort of cleverly sophomore *jeu d'esprit* that many twenty-year-olds might have written; it is for allowing it to be published that he is to be censured. Even *The Chronicle of Clemendy* (1888), a picaresque episodic novel heavily derivative of Balzac and Rabelais, is seriously flawed in its very conception. Machen—like Lovecraft in his poetry—here opens the Pandora's box of conscious archaism. The problem with it is that it can now be used only parodically or ironically: any attempt to present archaism as a serious aesthetic instrument must be done on the heroic scale of a William Morris (who, let us remember, nevertheless had very advanced political views) lest the author be accused of being either irrelevant or coy. The reason why the pseudo-archaism of the early Dunsany succeeds is that we are aware that it transparently masks a profoundly cynical and "modern" view of the world.

But the "Great Decade": of Machen's fictional output saw the writing of such work as "The Great God Pan," the episodic novel *The Three Imposters*, "The Inmost Light," *The Hill of Dreams*, the exquisite prose poems later collected as *Ornaments in Jade* (1924), the short novel *A Fragment of Life*, and "The White People," (*Hieroglyphics* was also written at this time, but published in 1902.) These works—plus, perhaps, the later novel *The Secret Glory*, published in 1922 but written apparently, around 1907—is all the Machen fiction that anyone need read.

There are two reasons why the rest of Machen's tales can be virtually ignored: first, he had by 1907 said whatever he had to say in fiction; and secondly, he had become a journalist. This was perhaps the single worst thing that could ever have happened to a writer like Machen. In his autobiographies Machen is endlessly fond of describing, with a sort of masochistic *frisson*, the infinite agonies he suffered in the writing of his early work. Draft after draft, euphoria followed by near-suicidal despair, were the preliminaries to such a toilsomely wrought work as *The Hill of Dreams*. But when Machen became precisely what he did not want to become, a "literary man"—first as columnist and reviewer for *The Academy* (1907-12), then as roving reporter for *The London Evening*

News (1910-21), and finally as columnist or voluminous contributor to *T. P.'s Weekly* (1908-28), *The Lyons Mail* (1919-23), *The Observer* (1926-37), and *The Independent* (1933-35)—he was forced to write rapidly and frequently. His earlier tormented scribbling gave way to an evil facility. And the result is that Machen no longer wrote *about* anything, he wrote *around* it. A style that had once been the jewelled distillation of anguish became the desultory meandering of a man who has grown too fond of his own literary voice. The reverence with which Machen was regarded in the twenties—especially in America, where Lovecraft, Vincent Starrett, James Branch Cabell, Carl Van Vechten (who has a charming digression on Machen in his novel *Peter Whiffle* (1922), and others all lauded him as an ignored genius—seems to have encouraged Machen consciously to cultivate the image of his "famous obscurity." In *Dog and Duck* (1924) he tries to make himself a twentieth-century Lamb; and other collections of his essays and journalism appeared—*Dreads and Drolls* (1926), *Notes and Queries* (1926), *The Glitter of the Brook* (1932). But Machen's essays are all too discursive to merit real greatness; they never deliver the substance their themes seem to promise.

In his fiction the journalistic tinge can be seen as early as *The Secret Glory*, a strange combination of polemic and mysticism. His war stories—those collected in *The Bowmen and Other Legends of the War* (1915) and the short novel *The Terror* (1917)—all appeared first in newspapers; they are all perfectly contentless save for one curious detail we shall study later on—the gradual breakdown of the distinction between fiction and nonfiction, as the fictional persona insidiously melds into the consciously autobiographical voice of the author. The novelette "The Great Return" (1915) may be the one instance where Machen's journalistic style "works" in carrying forward the theme of the story. The tale—also first serialised in *The London Evening News*—tells the story of the return of the Holy Grail to a small town in Wales; and the coldly repertorial narrative voice causes the miraculous incidents to stand out in even bolder relief.

Machen's subsequent fiction deserves little consideration. He wrote several stories for Cynthia Asquith's anthologies in the 1920s, wrote *The Green Round* (1933), a drearily verbose and unfocused rehashing of old themes, for his publisher Ernest Benn, wrote "N" for his later collection *The Cosy Room* (1936), and wrote all new stories for *The Children of the Pool* (1936). "The Cosy Room" is an effective little *conte cruel*, quite unlike anything Machen ever wrote, but for that reason quite unrelated philosophically to the rest of his output. One uncollected story, "The Dover Road" (1936), intended for *The Children of the Pool* but not published there, is perhaps the best of these late works. Although lengthy, it is a tautly written tale about the mysterious "appearance" of a man in a house when he was evidently many miles away; Machen leaves the matter an open question, but again the matter-of-fact tone of the narrative convinces.

One must be constantly making apologies for Machen: so much of his work consists either of total failures or inessential items. One of the stock defences is to argue for the "charm" of much of this inessential writing; but this attempted exoneration becomes, even in the mouths of his loyal defenders, an unintended patronising condemnation. The fact is that Machen was a profoundly *self-indulgent* writer. This is not merely to say that he wrote what he wished to write, without thought of popular success; this is no doubt true, as it is true of Lovecraft and Dunsany, and it is certainly a major cause of the strength and vigour of Machen's best work, from "The White People" to *The Secret Glory*. But Machen did not have the self-discipline to know when he was producing works of a totally ephemeral nature (*The Anatomy of Tobacco, Dr. Stiggins*) or works that said nothing new (*The Green Round*). His torrents of journalism—which easily dwarfs the whole of his fiction combined—can actually be excused on the ground that Machen needed the money (who reads the bulk of Poe's non-theoretical critical writings and reviews, written for precisely the same motive?) and on the ground that he made no effort to save this material for posterity. But when a man writes stories as arid and tired as those in *The Children of the Pool*, one must wonder what sort of self-awareness he had.

But it is not his poorest but his best work that an author must be judged—Machen makes the point again and again about Cervantes, whose *Don Quixote* is the only work of his that survives and deserves to survive. It is to the works of Machen which we fervently hope will survive that we turn our attention.

"Man is a sacrament, soul manifested under the form of body": this is the key to Machen's early horror stories, "The Great God Pan," *The Three Imposters*, "The Red Hand," "The Shining Pyramid," and "The White People." It is, in fact, interesting that Machen chose to render this notion in horrific terms, and he seems to provide the rationale for it in the celebrated passage from "The Red Hand" that Lovecraft cited as the epigraph to "The Horror at Red Hook":

> There are sacraments of evil as well as of good about us, and we live and move to my belief in an unknown world, a place where there are caves and shadows and dwellers in twilight. It is possible that man may sometimes return on the track of evolution, and it is my belief that an awful lore is not yet dead. [13]

The sacrament—the ritual whereby one establishes a mystic union with God—can be both sacred and sacrilegious; the breaking down of the barrier between soul and body can be both awesome and horrifying. This is the theme of "The Great God Pan": the experiment performed on the servant girl Mary is meant to span "the unutterable, the unthinkable gulf that yawns profound between two worlds, the world of matter and the world of spirit." [14] Put in these terms, the breach can only be horrific. Mary sees Pan—i.e., sees the world "as it really is," reality shorn of the material world which is nothing but a pallid symbol of reality—and promptly goes mad and afterward dies. Machen was quite consciously reviving, in the horrific mode, the ancient tale of Semele, who wished to see Zeus as he really was—as Hera saw him—not in the various disguises (swan, bull, shower of gold) by which he masked his awesome reality. She too is overwhelmed and transported to heaven.

But for all the powerful conceptions and symbolism Machen is suggesting here, the actual tale degenerates into a frenzied expression of horror over illicit sex. Machen's early readers knew this and reacted with the shock and disgust to be expected of late Victorian audiences. Machen, both in *Things Near and Far* and in that most unique book *Precious Balms* (where he merely reprints the unfavourable reviews he has received over his career, with very little comment—one of the most subtly satiric ploys he ever made), is fond of citing the horrified reactions of readers and reviewers alike. But in our day the issue has become tameness itself: we simply cannot regard aberrant sex as the "sin against Nature" that Machen evidently regarded it. Lovecraft, in an analysis far more acute than the panegyric of Machen he wrote in "Supernatural Horror in Literature," sensed this:

> People whose minds are—like Machen's—steeped in the orthodox myths of religion, naturally find the poignant

fascination in the conception of things which religion brands with outlawry and horror. Such people take the artificial and obsolete conception of "sin" seriously, and find it full of dark allurement . . . . The filth and perversion which to Machen's obsolete orthodox mind meant profound defiances of the universe's foundations, mean to us only a rather prosaic and unfortunate species of organic maladjustment—no more frightful, and no more interesting, than a headache, a fit of colic, or an ulcer on the big toe.[15]

What is more, "The Great God Pan" suffers from precisely the flaw which Machen (correctly) recognised in Stevenson's *Dr. Jekyll and Mr. Hyde*: once the secret is out, the tale falls flat:

On the surface it would seem to be merely sensationalism; I expect that when you read it you did so with breathless absorption, hurrying over the pages in your eagerness to find out the secret, and this secret once discovered I imagine that *Jekyll and Hyde* retired to your shelf—and stays there, rather dusty. You have never opened it again? Exactly. I *have* read it for a second time, and I was astonished to find how it had, if I may say so, evaporated.[16]

Similarly, once we know that the strange woman running through the various segments of the narrative is the same person—Helen Vaughan, daughter of Mary and "no mortal father", as Lovecraft quaintly put it—all our interest in the tale is gone. The story is in fact extremely clumsy in construction and is written in a horribly florid and stilted style that must have made Machen wince after he revamped his style in *The Hill of Dreams*. "The Great God Pan," then, is a profound failure for not actually delivering on what it promises. There are at least two stories derived from "The Great God Pan" that are considerably superior to it in the realisation of their goals—I refer to Lovecraft's "The Dunwich Horror" and Peter Straub's *Ghost Story*.[17]

The horror of sex is also the underlying theme of "The White People," otherwise a wonderful tale and easily Machen's most skillful horror story. Here again we are led to imagine something stupendously cosmic in the celebrated discussion of evil that introduces the tale:

"What would your feelings be, seriously, if your cat or your dog began to talk to you, and to dispute with you in human accents? You would be overwhelmed with horror. I am sure of it. And if the roses in your garden sang a weird song, you would go mad. And suppose the stones in the road began to swell and grow before your eyes, and if the pebble that you noticed at night had shot out stony blossoms in the morning?" [18]

But it does not seem that the tale itself carries out this notion, for it is simply the (admittedly mesmerising) story of a girl insidiously indoctrinated by her nurse into the witch-cult and the orgies she eventually practices. And yet, nothing could be more brilliant than the telling of this tale through the girl's perfectly ingenuous diary, where only a few telling hints—"I am going to write here many of the old secrets and some new ones, but there are some I shall not put down at all"[19]—that are both psychologically sound and shuddersomely suggestive. I wonder if many literary historians have noted the stupendous anticipation of stream-of-consciousness represented by this diary—we are still in 1899, years before the emergence of Dorothy Richardson and Virginia Woolf. This diary is a masterpiece of indirection—a Lovecraft plot told by James Joyce.

Machen's loathing of illicit sex crops up in two later stories that have no compensating innovations to redeem them, "The Bright Boy" and "The Children of the Pool." Both tales—but particularly the former—are marred by extreme ineptitude in narration. "The Bright Boy" would have been an effective tale of a hideous old man who yet retains the appearance of a young boy (thus representing a double dichotomy of youth vs. age and innocence vs. corruption) if Machen had not tacked on an intolerably prosy and needless explanation at the end which completely spoils the subtlety of the rest of the story. Machen had already indicated, by adroit hints, the nature of the situation, but could evidently resist spelling out the situation in black and white for his less astute readers. This sort of thing mars a number of Machen's tales—notably "The Shining Pyramid," otherwise a tepid rehashing of "The Red Hand"—and points to one of Machen's greatest failings as a fiction-writer: the lack of narrative skill. Machen's whole style, even at the beginning of his career, is the style of the essayist, not the fictionist—exposition, not narrative. In a way this accounts for the chatty introduc-

12

tions found frequently in Machen—notably "The White People": these passages, where two characters abstractly discuss an issue that proves to be the theme of the story, lay the intellectual groundwork for the actual narrative, which then becomes merely an instantiation of the general truth enunciated at the beginning. The technique, ironically, is that the empirical science that Machen held in such scorn: "The Great God Pan," "The Red Hand," "The Shining Pyramid," and "The White People" all form part of an empirical fund of data proving the proposition that the "Little People" exist.

Some words should be said about this "Little People Mythos," as it may be called. It seems to consist of the tales just mentioned, along with "The Novel of the Black Seal," "Out of the Earth," and perhaps "The Bright Boy." There is, of course, no question of any systematic unity in these tales, but there is still less question of Machen's actual belief in the former existence of such a race:

> Of recent years abundant proof has been given that a short, non-Aryan race once dwelt beneath ground, in hillocks, throughout Europe, their raths have been explored, and the weird old tales of green hills all lighted up at night have received confirmation. Much in the old legends may be explained by a reference to this primitive race. The stories of changelings, and captive women, become clear on the supposition that the "fairies" occasionally raided the houses of the invaders.[20]

This was written more than two decades before the publication of Margaret A. Murray's *The Witch-Cult in Western Europe* (1921), which gave the stamp of approval on the thesis. But Machen knew that the really adventuresome aspect of his theory—or, rather, the radical extension of it which he made for fictional purposes—was that "the People still lived in hidden caverns in wild and lonely lands", something he knew was "wildly impossible."[21] But behind all this speculative anthropology is the symbolism of the Little People. They are horrible and loathsome, to be sure, but they have at least one advantage over modern man—they have retained that primal sacrament (perverted, of course, by bestiality and violence) which links them with the Beyond. There is something of awe mingled with the horror experienced by the narrators when they witness the "Pyramid of Fire" summoned by the Little People in "The Shining Pyramid," and this signals the truth uttered by the protagonist of "The White People": "Sorcery and sanctity . . . these are

13

the only realities. each is an ecstasy, a withdrawal from the common life."[22]

It is worth while to linger over "The Novel of the Black Seal," since it not only is a magnificent horror tale but introduces another powerful symbol in the Machenian cosmos—the hieroglyph. Actually, it is merely a variation or substitute for the symbol of the veil, "which reveals what it conceals." The hieroglyph appears in this tale—in the form of the black seal itself, a small block of stone with inexplicable characters carved upon it—and also in "The Red Hand" and "The Shining Pyramid"; and its meaning is not always obvious. The hieroglyph conceals because it cannot be deciphered by ordinary (we are inclined to say profane) people; it reveals only to those—like Professor Gregg or Dyson—who have penetrated the veil. But what it half reveals is frightening simply because it suggests dimly a whole realm of entity not known to the world at large. Just as the Chinese language hints cloudily (to those who do not know Chines) of the whole world of Chinese literature, history, and society, so too the weird hieroglyphs on the black seal imply the existence of an evil culture on the underside (quite literally) of civilisation. In "The White People" we have a slight variation of the hieroglyph theme—the strange references to the "Aklo letters," the "Chian language," the "Mao games," and the like. These are *verbal hieroglyphs*, and they too only hint (to the uninitiated) of an unsuspected civilisation with its own rituals, its own language, its own customs. the horror is not simply that this civilisation seems to be barbaric and vicious, but that it exists at all: how could such a culture remain an unfathomed mystery all this time? We are suddenly forced to question our own apparent dominance of the world.

We have alluded to "The Novel of the Black Seal" and spoken of it as an independent ale; and although Machen frequently did the same, we must recall that this tale, as well as Machen's other famous story "The Novel of the White Powder," were originally printed in the strange episodic novel *The Three Imposters* (1985). But this is no incoherent jumble as many of, say, Robert W. Chambers's episodic novels—really short stories bunglingly stitched together for marketing purposes—are; although "The Novel of the Iron Maid" was written independently (and incorporated deftly into the fabric of the novel), and other "novels" ("Black Seal," White Powder," "Dark Valley") were written as integral components of *The Three Imposters*. At this stage we need not dwell on Machen's aesthetically fatal attempt to imitate Stevenson—whose *New Ara-*

bian Nights and *The Dynamiters* provided the episodic framework of *The Three Imposters* as well as the atrociously flippant narrative tone—and there is something to be said for the view of some early reviewers that Machen has out-Stevensoned Stevenson. The real key to the novel lies in its subtitle (irksomely omitted from the Knopf reprint), *The Transmutations*. For all four of the "novels" (= the French *nouvelle*, tale) present transmutations in various ways. On one level we are concerned with a transmutation of landscape— from the suburbs of London ("Iron Maid," "White Powder") to the "wild, domed hills" of Wales ("Black Seal") to the desolate wilderness of the American West ("Dark Valley"). The transmutation of human beings from ordinary citizens to something akin to daemons occurs in "Dark Valley" and "Iron Maid," while a physical transmutation of the most hideous sort is the subject of "White Powder." But there are more profound transmutations going on here. When the narrator of "Black Seal" remarks that "I read the key to the awful transmutation of the hills,"[23] she is not referring to scenery: she is referring to the transformation of her conception of what lies behind and within those hills in light of the knowledge of the Little People unearthed by Professor Gregg; this is declared explicitly by the doctor who treats the hapless victim of "White Powder": "My old conception of the universe has been swept away."[24] This is the ultimate transmutation.

And yet, we too have now been guilty of treating the "novels" in *The Three Imposters* as separate entities. What happens when we restore them to their contexts? The result, curiously, is not only comic but profoundly ironic. the fact is that these "novels" are narrated by one or another of "three impostors," whose sole purpose is to capture and kill the "young man with spectacles" who flits through the novel like a frightened fawn; in the end they succeed in disposing of him in a particularly grisly way. The result is that these tales are all (in the context of the novel) *complete fabrications*, designed only to trick the two protagonists, Dyson and Phillipps, who hear the stories, into leading them to the spectacled young man. Machen slyly hints at this at the conclusion of "White Powder," when he says that Dyson "decided that he would abjure all Milesian and Arabian methods of entertainment"[25]—a Milesian tale being, in antiquity, what we would call a tall tale. I confess I do not know what Machen is trying to get at in thus undercutting his own work in this fashion. All I can fathom is that he is ridiculing the whole modern tendency of literary realism. His "novels"

15

. are certainly to be classified in the category of "supernatural realism," where all events are described in a background of meticulous realism of scene, character, and psychological motivation. It is as if Machen is saying that this realism is really only a grotesque joke in light of the awesome mystery of the cosmos.

I have saved the discussion of "The Inmost Light," a relatively early story, for last, since it provides a transition from Machen's tales of horror to what might be termed his tales of awe and wonder. "The Inmost Light," although it uses the mechanism of a scientific experiment like that found in "The Great God Pan" and makes a use of coincidence even more flagrantly implausible than in that story—something Machen lamely defended in "The Red Hand" by the "theory of improbability"), it is not so much horrifying as transcendental. It is true that a death occurs—the scientist's wife, the subject of the experiment—but her parting is handled with a tenderness and elegance far from the elemental expiring of Helen Vaughan. What is the nature of the experiment here? It is nothing more than the separation of soul from body; and there is awe in the success of this experiment, as the soul is dislodged from the woman into an opal:

> But on the table the opal flamed and sparkled with such light as no eyes of man have ever gazed on, and the rays of the flame that was within it flashed and glittered, and shown even to my heart.[26]

That light—the inmost light—is the soul. Light and fire are, for Machen, powerful symbols, because they are the most immaterial of material objects, and as such symbolize for him the union of matter and spirit, body and soul.

This dualism extends beyond the individual: in a social dimension it is symbolized by the alienation of the sensitive man (the "soul") from a crass and materialistic society (the "body"). This sort of dualism is at the heart of some of Machen's most ethereal works, *A Fragment of Life, The Hill of Dreams,* and *The Secret Glory.* Some shorter tales anticipate the trend. In many of the prose poems collected in *Ornaments in Jade* (written in 1897, but published only in 1924) we find anticipations of the great loners that populate Machen's novels. "The Idealist" is an exquisite example, telling of a man who leads the prosy life of a clerk by day but ventures into his own world of imagination by night. The title is particularly apt in that it suggests the conventional philosophical opposition of

16

idealism and materialism. A character in "Psychology" makes the matter explicit:

> "And every day," he went on, "we lead two lives, and the half of our soul is madness, and half heaven is lit by a black sun. I say I am a man, but who is the other that hides in me?"[27]

In other stories in this collection the point is made in another way. In "The Ceremony," "Midsummer," and others we are presented glimpses of otherwise "normal" people who—sometiems without even being aware of it—are found to practise the most ancient and primitive of rituals. However brutalised men are by the dominant materialism of the age, their sense of spirituality can well up in spite of themselves in the practise of these sacraments. "The White People" displays this idea in the horrific mode, but in the *Ornaments* collection the notion of ritual is nothing but an ecstasy. All these tales are vignettes, but they can be nothing more; as prose poems they stand as some of the finest in the language.

It is worth discussing the short novel *A Fragment of Life* here, since, although it was written after *The Hill of Dreams*, it carries on the sense of ecstasy in common things which typifies the *Ornaments in Jade*. Some passages in the autobiographies are helpful in showing Machen's change of direction from horror to awe and wonder. Of "The Great God Pan" he remarks: "Here . . . was my real failure; I translated awe, at worst awefulness, into evil."[28] Elsewhere we find what is the real heart of the story:

> And it is utterly true that he who cannot find wonder, mystery, awe, the sense of a new world and an undiscovered realm in the places by the Gray's Inn Road will never find those secrets elsewhere, not in the heart of Africa, not in the fabled hidden cities of Tibet.[29]

This would not seem at all what is going on in *A Fragment of Life* as we read its opening pages: in this story of Edward Darnell, an ordinary city clerk, and his wife we might—save for the British setting—imagine that we have stumbled into a social novel by Edith Warton or Louis Auchincloss. But the very ordinariness of their lives--spent discussing the furnishing of the spare room, the reception of guests, the monotonous coming and going to and from work—is vital to establish the fact that, "day after day [Darnell] lived in the grey phantasmal world, akin to death, that has, somehow, with most of us, made good its claim to be called life."[30] To be sure, Darnell—and still more his wife—are (as we must call them in our post-Freudian age) repressed; not merely sexually repressed, but repressed in their very inability to communicate to each other—or even to realize clearly to themselves—their love, their awe, their ecstasy. The material world has crushed them—socially, financially, emotionally; as Machen says poignantly elsewhere, "It was all a very small life."[31]

But as the novel progresses Darnell imperceptibly begins to step back and realize the vacuity of this stolid material existence; he hears the call of his Welsh heritage, and at the end he and his wife return to a fuller life in Wales. But the alteration is more than that of mere scenery: through his new vision of the world even prosy London is transformed:

> London seemed a city of the Arabian Nights, and its labyrinths of streets an enchanted maze; its long avenues of lighted lamps were as starry systems, and its immensity became for him an image of the endless universe. He could well imagine how pleasant it might be to linger in such a world as this, to sit apart and dream, beholding the strange pageant played before him; but the Sacred Well was not for common use, it was for the cleansing of the soul, and the healing of the grievous wounds of the spirit. There must be yet another transformation: London had become Bagdad; it must at last be transmuted to Syon, or in the phrase of one of his old documents, the City of the Cup.[32]

But the miracle of this novel is its absolute seamlessness: it is impossible to tell when or how this transition in Darnell has occurred; he can simply conclude that he was

> filled with the thought of that far-off summer day, when some enchantment had informed all common things, transmuting them into a great sacrament, causing earthly works to glow with the fire and the glory of the everlasting light.[33]

This is the Machen we love and admire: the writer who can invest the ordinary with a sense of numinous wonder. We know that the material world was for Machen only the crude symbol for something greater, something more transcendent; and he has never more flawlessly realized that conception than in *A Fragment of Life*.

18

Without the least violence in diction or incident, it is as violent a condemnation of late Victorian social *mores* as Butler's *The Way of All Flesh*; and I suspect, too, that Machen with this work was wanting to show his contemporaries how a real "social novel" should be written. But, more than mere social satire or literary polemic, *A Fragment of Life* strives to awake us all to the beauty and mystery of things. It is Machen's most finished and satisfying work.

Both *The Hill of Dreams* and *The Secret Glory* are marred by their oily and transparent sarcasm, a strange thing for Machen to do if we are to believe his condemnation of satire in art:

> Art, you may feel quite assured, proceeds always from love and rapture, never from hatred and disdain, and satire of every kind *qua* satire is eternally condemned to that Gehenna where the pamphlets, the "literature of the subject," and the "life-like" books lie all together.[34]

But the satire in both these novels is more or less integral to them, as establishing the contrast to the delicate aestheticism of the central characters. Of *The Hill of Dreams*, that rich and disturbing book, it is impossible to say too much; and I shall concentrate on only a few features of it. Of course, the theme is that of the artist's spiritual loneliness; as he says in *Hieroglyphics*, "I think that real literature has always been produced by men who have preserved a certain loneliness of soul, if not of body."[35] But what strikes me as most interesting about this novel is its apparently ambiguous conclusion. Throughout the novel we are presented with Lucian Taylor's agonizing attempts to capture on paper his emotions about "the form and mystery of the domed hills"[36]; and while he attempts to do so both in his native Wales and in his London garret, he seems ultimately to fail, for he dies of a drug overdose and his landlady finds the pitiful remnants of his work:

> She spread the neat pile of manuscript broadcast over the desk, and took a sheet at haphazard. It was all covered with illegible hopeless scribblings; only here and there it was possible to recognize a word.[37]

Is Lucian, then a failed artist? In a sense yes, but that failure was inevitable and brought on by his—and, by extension, all true artists'—relation to society. It is not merely that what Lucian had to say was "occult," in the literal sense of the word—hidden (from the mass of humanity); it is that, as Lucian's life progresses, his art

19

compels him into a more and more profound misanthropy. Lucian cannot write coherently because he has lost the desire to communicate to his fellow-creatures; "he realized that he had lost the art of humanity forever."[38] His earlier attempts at writing are instructive in this regard: as a young man he produces a manuscript and naively sends it to a publisher in London; it is tactfully rejected, but some months later a work by a celebrated novelist appears embodying much of the text of Lucian's novel. For a time this angers him, but he later shrugs it off as meaningless:

> He had tried hard to write, chiefly, it is true, from love of the art, but a little from a social motive. He had imagined that a written book and the praise of respectable journals would ensure him the respect of the country people.[39]

He comes to realize that all this is vanity, that "the love of art dissociated man from the race."[40]

In his way Ambrose Meyrick, the hero of Machen's other novel *The Secret Glory*, is as misanthropic as Lucian Taylor, but his misanthropy is manifested in a wholly different manner. There are very puzzling questions as to the genesis of this work, and matters are in some ways made worse if we read Machen's "true" ending of the novel—a manuscript of 143 leaves currently deposited in the Yale University Library with instructions by Machen that it never be published. Why he should have issued such a peculiar decree is unfathomable, for without these two final chapters the novel is seriously disfigured—Machen's hasty precis of the events of these chapters in the published "Epilogue" to the book is worse than useless. But although this unpublished ending contains some of Machen's richest prose, it does not help much to lend any sense of unity to the novel. the work oscillates from a vicious satire from the British school system to a languid description of Meyrick's sense of wonder and mystery. In reality these are two sides of the same coin, as Machen hints in one of his articles:

> Reality is only to be apprehended by the imaginative faculty; and it is because this truth is not appreciated that the whole of modern education is not only useless, but poisonous and disastrous; and even from the "practical" point of view a hideous and expensive failure.[41]

Here again what we may call Machen's "social dualism"—materialistic society against the sensitive individual is the core of the story, but there is a deepening of the idea here. Meyrick's own native country of Wales takes on the qualities of "soul" that he denies to the horrible school of Lupton where he drags out his unprofitable terms: Meyrick speaks of

> that land where flame was the most material substance; whose inhabitants dwell in palpitating and quivering colours or in the notes of a wonderful melody.[42]

Meyrick's misanthropy, conversely, is carried out in a more traditional fashion than Lucian's: Meyrick begins to "play the game," and do all that the crass and stolid headmaster expects of him—playing cricket and rugby, working with apparent enthusiasm on the mindless exercises—but then, after a wild vacation in London with the servant girl Nelly, he refuses to go up to Oxford and instead joins a touring acting company. This—along with his mystic return to his homeland, where he retrieves the sacred cup of Tielo Sant and then suffers "Red Martyrdom" in Asia—is the substance of the two unpublished chapters of the novel.

But the work does not hang together. the book is too unfocused, too desultory in its narration, and Machen is too fond of making lengthy detours to attack the various aspects of modern civilization that offend him. The many parallels we find with *The Hill of Dreams*—Meyrick's romance with Nelly and, later, with the Welsh girl Sylvia, similar to Lucian's perfectly chaste worship of the country girl Annie; Meyrick's perception that London has an Arabian Nights atmosphere;[43] his sense of detachment from humanity—give the impression that Machen's imagination is running thin. In a sense this work is more self-indulgent than anything he has written, and we can read it only if we are in sympathy with those things that Machen favours and are opposed to those he randomly attacks.

But we can read this novel—as we can nearly the whole of Machen—for nothing but the beauty of its style. One passage will suffice, and I quote from the unpublished section of *The Secret Glory* describing Ambrose's and Sylvia's wanderings over the Welsh countryside:

> It was not many days before Sylvia and he saw in each other's eyes the completion of earthly desires. Sylvia's father, busied with his books and papers, sent them out together in the fields and woods, and often all the day they

were together, searching out old paths and new, wandering far over the hills, pressing up the steep sides of the mountain, alone on the endless waste of the summit, severed it seemed from all the turmoil of the world on that wild high plain, set with grim limestone rocks, where the unceasing wind sang as it were with the strings of a great harp. Or there were lower heights all aflower with thickets of golden gorse, and here in some sheltered cove of the unshorn bushes they would rest in the sunlight, hearing the clear wind and the clearer lark above them, in that fine and delicate air, scented with the multitude of the yellow blossoms. They loved to find these hidden places, to which sometimes narrow paths, worn by the sheep, led with many and intricate windings, like the turnings and returnings of a labyrinth, and once within the heart of the maze they would sit at ease, alone with one another, speaking of many things, while the white clouds floated across the sky, and the high wind sang.[44]

This passage is one of many that fulfills Machen's own ideas on style: "It may be like an ingeniously devised cryptogram, which may have an occult sense conveyed to initiated eyes in every dot and line and flourish, but is outwardly as simple and straightforward as a business letter."[45] There is no sentence in Machen which we need read twice; it is all as clear as a limpid pool—but a pool that hides singular things under its placid surface.

Machen's fiction after *The Secret Glory* is one long succession of failures. Some think highly of *The Terror*, but it is in fact unspeakably bad. The American magazine *The Century* printed a shortened version of the short novel—reduced to a mere quarter of its size—which is a significant improvement on the original; and it would be rather better for Machen's reputation if this version were better known. As it is, the novel contains many absurdities. The premise—the animals revolting from man—is clever, but, as with The Great God Pan," the tale is intolerably flat once this premise is known. At the conclusion Machen presents us with two hypotheses to account for the revolt: either the creatures were affected by a "contagion of hate" because of the war, or the animals felt that man had abdicated his spiritual role as lord of creation by sinking too deeply into materialism. Of course, Machen adopts the latter solution; in which case we are led to wonder why the creatures didn't revolt either during the heyday of Bacon and Hobbes—the founders of modern materialism—or during the Industrial Revolution. And few rationalists will be alarmed by Machen's statement that the paradox of Achilles and the tortoise (refuted 2300 years ago by Aristotle) proves that "all science is a lie"!

As it is, the most interesting thing about Machen's later stories is what appears to be a systematic breakdown of the distinction between fiction and nonfiction. This would seem to link him to some very recent literary trends, but it hardly need be said that the relation is accidental—or at least much more accidental than his anticipation of stream-of-consciousness in "The White People." The trend seems to begin with some of the war stories: "The Dazzling Light" begins very like on of Machen's essays, with their urbane chattiness and negligence to come very quickly to the point. "Munitions of War" and "Out of the Earth" make no secret of the fact that the narrator is not a fictional persona but Machen himself— Machen the author of "The Bowmen" (mentioned in both stories), Machen the reporter. In "The Great Return" a character confronts Machen with the following:

> "I know you are a railer," he said, and the phrase coming from this mild old gentleman astonished me unutterably. "You are a railer and a bitter railer; I have read articles that you have written, and I know your contempt and your hatred for those you call Protestants in your derision; though your grandfather, the vicar of Caerleon-on-Usk, called himself Protestant and was proud of it, and your great-grand-uncle Hezekiah, *ffeiriad coch yr Castletown*— the Red Priest of Castletown—was a great man with the Methodists of his day, and the people flocked by their thousands when he administered the sacrament."[46]

We know from Machen's autobiographies that this is all true, although for this story Machen the narrator adopts a slightly greater tone of scepticism and incredulity than he probably felt, so as to emphasize the miraculous events of the tale—events so unlike what one would expect to find in the columns of a newspaper, where this and the other tales I have mentioned appeared.

Is there a point to this mingling of author and persona—or, rather, the utter disinclination to establish a viable persona distinct from the author? One might be tempted to reply that by this time

Machen, feeling himself to be a great man of letters, simply could not bother to create a fictional narrator different from himself—that, like Byron, he felt the force of his own personality would carry the narrative forward. This answer is unsatisfactory for two reasons: first, these stories were written in a period (1914-15) preceding Machen's transatlantic fame as a Great Cham of Letters; and secondly, one suspects that, for all the false modesty Machen exhibits elsewhere, he simply would not have obtruded himself into his stories out of sheer arrogance. We would be closer to the truth if we suspected that these tales—knowingly designed for newspaper publication, where the very context would augment their credibility as fact, not fiction—were consciously planned *hoaxes*. I think there is something to be said for this view; and yet, in the end, this explanation may have to give way to a broader one—one that has been implicit in much of what I have already said. In my analysis of Machen's philosophy I had no hesitation in drawing upon Machen's tales—even those where he himself is not the obvious narrator—for examples of his views on life and letters. This can be done with relative insouciance for the simple reason that Machen's tales are not merely outgrowths of his philosophy—as Lovecraft knew his tales were—but are, like his essays, part and parcel of his grand attempt to promote his mystical view of life. The tales are as polemical as his essays, and one suspects that Machen has adopted this method of hectoring his contemporaries because he found that his actual polemics—like *Dr. Stiggins*, which feel stillborn from the press—were not proving very effective. Materialism was still on the rampage, even in the wake of the cultural devastation brought on by World War I; and so Machen would insidiously convince his readers that the strange and wonderful and non-materialistic things that happen in these stories—for they are hardly more than peculiar incidents not amenable to rationalistic explanation, and are told with scarcely any "artistry" in the traditional senses of narrative skill, character portrayal, and mood development—actually did happen.

So Machen's later fiction reads like nonfiction; and similarly, his nonfiction—we are now talking of his autobiographies, *Far Off Things* (1922), *Things Near and Far* (1923), and *The London Adventure* (1924), and certain other pieces—bear unmistakable fictional traits. We are, of course, long past the stage of being able to regard an autobiography as simply the "naked truth" about its author. The mere act of selection and the adoption of a given tone point to devices not far from fiction. And in the case of Machen it can be seen that he is carefully manipulating and moulding the only character—namely, himself—he could ever portray realistically and sympathetically. I need not remark that there is no implication here of conscious deception: Machen is not trying to falsify himself. But he is being remarkably selective. In the whole of his three auto-biographies, for example, we find only two fleeting mentions of his two wives and children; one mention so oblique—"Then a great sorrow which had long been threatened fell upon me: I was once more alone"[47]—that we would not know what the reference was (since Machen had up to this point not mentioned his wife at all) unless we knew independently that Machen's first wife was long afflicted with cancer and finally died in 1899. We hear randomly of Machen's friends and associates, but only sporadically and anecdotally—as in the charming remark, "Oscar Wilde confessed to me once, with shame be it said, that he thought absinthe a detestable drink."[48] But on the whole the impression we get is of a poor, solitary man living on bread, green tea, and tobacco, and writing, in the loneliness of his attic garret, curious and eccentric works that no one wants to read.

But haven't we heard this before? Is this not Lucian Taylor of *The Hill of Dreams?* It is impossible to determine whether Machen is Lucian or Lucian is Machen; their personalities have fused. Indeed, I must admit that one of the most harrowing things Machen ever wrote is not a story at all but merely the preface to the Knopf edition of *The Hill of Dreams.* In an act that comes close to self-flagellation—and is uncannily similar to Lucian's own self-mutilation for the sake of his beloved—Machen describes in agonizing detail the painful gestation of his great novel: the long year and a half of writing and rewriting, of elation followed by the despair of having followed a false trail:

> Alas! My pride had a deep fall indeed. I read over those last three chapters and saw suddenly that they were all hopelessly wrong, that they would not do at any price, that I had turned, unperceiving, from the straight path by ever so little, and had gone on, getting farther and farther away from the true direction till the way was hopelessly lost. I was in the middle of a black wood and I could not see any path out of it.
>
> There was only one thing to be done. The three condemned chapters went into the drawer and I began over

again from the end of Chapter Four. Five and Six were done, and then again I struggled desperately for many weeks, trying to find the last chapter. False tracks again, hopeless efforts, spoilt folios thick about me till by some chance or another, I know not how, the right notion was given me, and I wrote the seventh and last chapter in a couple of nights. Once more the thought of the old land had come to my help; the book was finished. It had occupied form first to last the labour of eighteen months.[49]

"The thought of the old land" is similarly what sustains Lucian through his own despair. And Machen cannot help adding that, once his book was finished, it was sent to a publisher, who rejected it politely but announced shortly thereafter a novel very like *The Hill of Dreams* by someone else (this novel, evidently, was never published). If this is true, it may make one believe in the super- · natural, since this whole event is a duplicate of the incident in chapter two of *The Hill of Dreams*.

Throughout these three autobiographies, but especially in *The London Adventure*, Machen not merely talks about his writing, but—somewhat disingenuously—admits to never fulfilling on paper the visions in his mind (the poignant "He dreamed in fire; he has worked in clay"[50]) and also to the works he could have liked to write. Indeed, the whole *London Adventure* is about Machen's not having written a book called *The London Adventure*. The work begins by Machen's determination to write of the magic and mystery of London; it is a refrain that structures the whole book, but at the same time Machen confesses that what he is actually writing is not that work but something else, similar to it but inferior. At the conclusion Machen admits to his failure:

So here ends, without beginning, *The London Adventure*; and, indeed, I have been in London all this summer of 1923. I had thought of calling the book "The Curate's Egg," but I have a distaste for boastful titles.[51]

The self-deprecation is typical, and accounts for another curious feature of the work: Machen's copious reproductions from a juvenile notebook or commonplace book. The keeping of a commonplace book is not unusual—we hardly need recall the use Lovecraft made of his—but the conscious publication of it in an autobiography is a statement of a particular sort. Machen's commonplace book is certainly intrinsically fascinating—full of hints of strange stories never written, notes for *The Hill of Dreams, A Fragment of Life,* and other works—but it is the more interesting because of Machen's deliberate invitation of the reader into his own creative process. In a certain way the displaying of his unwritten story notes absolves Machen from actually having to write the story—from the threat of working in clay what he dreamed in fire—since the reader is compelled to exercise his own imagination in conceiving what the story might have been like; in effect, the reader writes the story. At the same time, our criticism of Machen for not having realized his vision is disarmed by his own confessions of incompetence:

> And so I run through the old notebook, through dozens of these "hints" and "sketches" and "outlines" and "arguments," most of which led to nothing in particular. I find it all a little pathetic, and a little puzzling. I find my destiny a hard one. Here am I, born apparently with this itch of writing without the faculty of carrying the desire into execution . . . . I dig deep, I burrow, far under the ground, I hew out my laborious subterranean passages, I blast whole strata of unsuspected rocks which suddenly interpose themselves between me and my end, I dwell down in that stiffling blackness of toil, month after month, year after year, scarcely emerging to see the light of the sun and the glow of the green world. At last, after all these dark and dreadful labours, I succeed in laying my mine. I touch the button—and there is a feeble pop, which would hardly make a kitten jump.[52]

This goes beyond the level of modesty and becomes comic exaggeration. Lest I be misunderstood, let me make clear that I am not doubting that Machen did indeed sincerely feel that he rarely if ever succeeded in fulfilling his vision; but this degree of self-abasement is more than a little puzzling. And it all contributes to a very specific image of Machen the man and writer which he very carefully wishes us to have.

But Machen is not a liar; and even though, in the passage just quoted, he continues to fashion what must now (in 1923) be the myth of his toilsome efforts at writing, it is because we know Machen to be in fact describing himself that these works gain their delicate poignancy. The magic of his autobiographies lies in the seriocomic way in which Machen tells of the real misery and privation he suffered in his life, as in the description of his small room at Clarendon Road in the early 1880s:

> It was, of course, at the top of the house, and it was much smaller than any monastic "cell" that I have ever seen. From recollection I should estimate its dimensions as ten feet by five. It held a bed, a washstand, a small table, and one chair; and so it was very fortunate that I had few visitors. Outside, on the landing, I kept my big wooden box with all my possessions—and these not many—in it. And there was a very notable circumstance about this landing. On the wall was suspended, lengthwise, a step-ladder by which one could climb through a trap door to the roof in case of fire, and so between the rungs or steps of this ladder I disposed my library. For anything I know, the books tasted as well thus housed as they did at a later period when I kept them in an eighteenth-century bookcase of noble dark mahogany, behind glass doors. There was no fireplace in my room, and I was often very cold. I would sit in my shabby old great-coat, reading or writing, and if I were writing I would every now and then stand up and warm my hands over the gas-jet, to prevent my fingers getting numb.[53]

These works may be as rambling and discursive as many of his tales and essays; but that is Machen's prerogative in autobiography. In a real sense they have contributed and continue to contribute to his endurance as a writer; it is their very vividness in depicting Machen that makes us know that he is the central character of every one of his fictions.

A question of some interest is whether Machen is to be considered a "horror writer" at all. It does not appear as if he thought himself such. He derisively dismisses *The Terror* as "a 'shilling shocker'",[54] but does not strictly speaking discuss his works in the context of horror or fantasy literature. He certainly had a lifelong regard for Poe, and he was occasionally called on to review other writers now considered horror or science fiction writers—H. G. Wells, Walter de la Mare, Montague Summers' *The Supernatural Omnibus*. But if we do not call Machen a horror writer, it is because the genre as such did not exist in the time (1890s) and place (England) in which he wrote his major work. Lovecraft, who died a decade before Machen, was conscious of working in the horror tradition, because post-World War I America was already laying the groundwork for the segregation of horror fiction as a separate genre through the emergence of the pulp magazines. Whether such a segregation has been a good thing, either for horror or for literature, is a question I shall not enter upon, save to note that the distinction—now having become purely a marketing phenomenon—seems to be breaking down as far as "high" literature is concerned. But in England the segregation of horror came at a still later date, and if Machen is to be drafted into the genre, it will be strictly *ex post facto.* The ghost story, of course, is a distinct phenomenon having much older roots, but the sense of its whimsicalness which even its most eminent practitioner—M. R. James—regarded that subgenre separates it vastly from Machen's archetypal horrors.

But the question of genre can really only be decided by examining the manner in which a given author regards his own work. I think I have demonstrated that Machen's fiction is in every way an extension of his anti-materialistic polemic; and as such it—ironically—resembles those very "novels of purpose" (whose pre-eminent practitioner was George Eliot) that Machen claimed to despise. The fact is that much of Machen's fiction fails because it is too coldly calculative and subordinate to his intellectual preoccupations; and only those works that either fulfil his purposes perfectly--*A Fragment of Life*—or by their own dynamism escape Machen's conscious control—"The White People," *The Hill of Dreams*—really live as literature. In sum, only "The Great God Pan," "The White People," and *The Three Imposters* (I choose to ignore the bulk of his later fiction) can be classified as works of horror. *A Fragment of Life* and *The Hill of Dreams* have a pervasive strangeness to them, but so does the *Satyricon.* Machen's influence upon subsequent fantaisistes—Lovecraft, Bradbury, T. E. D. Klein—is undeniable; and one supposes that, at least in the short run, the care of his reputation rests in the hands of horror aficionados. Whether he will ever again attract a mainstream audience is difficult to say;' I honestly suspect not, and I also suspect that Machen would have wanted it that way. I think he enjoyed his position as a literary curiosity—in the manner of a Thomas Lovell Beddoes, a Poe, a Lafcadio Hearn—and he would have wished to appeal only to a small band of sympathetic readers. He knew he was a minor writer, and he relished it.

Appendix
Chronology of Machen's Fiction

I have tried to list here all the genuine stories of Machen (for some works it is difficult to tell whether we are to regard them as fiction or nonfiction), the dates of writing (approximate or conjectural in some cases), date of first publication, and—for works not separately published—date of first appearance in a collection of Machen's works. In the latter case I have assigned numbers to the nine volumes that contain first book appearances of stories.

Title	Date Written	First Published	First Collected
The Chronicle of Clemendy	1885-86	1888	1988
The Great God Pan	1890	1890	1894(1)
A Double Return	1890	1934	1936(8)
A Wonderful Woman	1890	1890	1923(4)
The Lost Club	1890	1890	1923(4)
An Underground Adventure	1890?	1890	—
The Three Impostors¹	(1890-) 1894	(1890-) 1895	1895
The Inmost Light	1892	1894	1894(1)
The Red Hand	1895	1895	1906(2)
The Shining Pyramid	1895	1895	1923(4)
The Hill of Dreams	1895-97	1904	1907
The Rose Garden	1897	1908	1924(5)
The Holy Things	1897	1908	1924(5)
The Turanians	1897	1924	1924(6)
The Idealist	1897	1924	1924(6)
Witchcraft	1897	1924	1924(6)
The Ceremony	1897	1924	1924(6)
Psychology	1897	1908	1924(6)
Torture	1897	1924	1924(5)
Midsummer	1897	1924	1924(6)
Nature	1897	1908	1923(4)
The White People	1899	1904	1906(2)
A Fragment of Life	1899-1904	1904	1906(2)
The Secret Glory²	1907	1907f.	1922
The Bowmen	1914	1914	1915(3)
The Soldiers' Rest	1914	1914	1914(3)
The Monstrance	1914	1915	1915(3)
The Dazzling Light	1914	1915	1915(3)
The Great Return	1915	1911	1915
Munitions of War	1915	1926	1936(8)

Out of the Earth	1915?	1915	1923(4)
The Terror	1916	1916	1917
The Happy Children	1920?	1920	1925(7)
The Islington Mystery	1927	1927	1936(8)
The Gift of Tongues	1927	1927	1936(8)
The Cosy Room	1928	1928	1936(8)
Johnny Double	1928?	1928	—
Awaking	1930	1930	1936(8)
Opening the Door	1931	1931	1936(8)
The Green Round	1932	1933	1933
Compliments of the Season	1934	1834	1936(8)
N	1935	1936	1936(8)
The Exalted Omega	1935	1936	1936(9)
The Children of the Pool	1935	1936	1936(9)
The Bright Boy	1935	1936	1936(9)
The Tree of Life	1935	1936	1936(9)
Out of the Picture	1935	1936	1936(9)
Change	1935	1936	1936(9)
The Dover Road	1935?	1937	—
Ritual	1937?		—

Collections of Machen's stories:
(1) *The Great God Pan* and *The Inmost Light* (1894)
(2) *The House of Souls* (1906)
(3) *The Bowmen and Other Legends of the War* (1915)
(4) *The Shining Pyramid*, ed. Vincent Starrett (1923)
(5) *The Glorious Mystery*, ed. Vincent Starrett (1924)
(6) *Ornaments in Jade* (1924)
(7) *The Shining Pyramid* (Secker, 1925)
(8) *The Cosy Room* (1936)
(9) *The Children of the Pool* (1936)

1 "The Novel of the Iron Maid" was written and published in 1890 and later incorporated into *The Three Imposters*.

2 Chapter 6 (unpublished) of *The Secret Glory* makes extensive use of a story or article titled "The Hidden Mystery," first published in 1907 but dated by Machen to 1897 when he reprinted it in *The Cosy Room*.

NOTES

1. *Hieroglyphics* (New York: Knopf, 1923), pp. 18-19.
2. Ibid., p. 73.
3. "Machen: A Biographical Study," in Brocard Sewell, ed., *Arthur Machen* (Llandeilo: St. Albert's Press, 1970), p. 13.
4. *The Secret Glory* (London: Secker, 1922), p. 186.
5. *Hieroglyphics*, pp. 124-25.
6. *Far Off Things* (London: Secker, 1922), pp. 104-5.
7. *The Children of the Pool* (London: Hutchinson, 1936), p. 210.
8. Ibid., p. 212.
9. Letter to Munson Havens, 1924; *A Few Letters from Arthur Machen* (Cleveland: Rowfant Club, 1932), p. 25.
10. *Hieroglyphics*, p. 27.
11. "Farewell to Materialism," *American Mercury*, 36 (September 1935), p. 51.
12. "Our Betty's Day OUt," *The Graphic*, March 14 and 21, 1925, pp. 404, 425; "The Mystery of a Century," *T. P.'s and Cassell's Weekly*, June 27 and July 3, 1926, pp. 311-12 and 351.
13. *The Three Imposters* (New York: Knopf, 1923), p. 255.
14. *The House of Souls* (New York: Knopf, 1922), p. 172.
15. Letter to Bernard Austin Dwyer, 1932; *Selected Letters 1932-1934*, ed. August Derleth and James Turner (Sauk City, WI: Arkham House, 1976), p. 4.
16. *Hieroglyphics*, pp. 70-71.
17. Straub has admitted the Machen influence on his novel in an interview in *Twilight Zone*, May 1981, p. 13.
18. *The House of Souls*, p. 116.
19. Ibid, p. 125.
20. "Folklore and Legends of the North," *Literature*, 24 September 1898, p. 272.
21. "On Re-reading *The Three Imposters* and the Wonder Story," unpublished ms., State Historical Society of Wisconsin.
22. *The House of Souls*, p. 113.
23. *The Three Imposters* (London: John Lane, 1895), p. 154.
24. Ibid., p. 233.
25. Ibid., p. 243.
26. *The House of Souls*, p. 286.
27. *Ornaments in Jade* (New York: Knopf, 1924), p. 27.
28. *Far Off Things* (London: Secker, 1922), p. 123.
29. *Things Near and Far* (New York: Knopf, 1923), p. 81.

30. *The House of Souls*, p. 35.
31. *The London Adventure* (London: Secker, 1924), p. 51.
32. *The House of Souls*, pp. 103-4.
33. Ibid., p. 43.
34. *Hieroglyphics*, p. 95.
35. Ibid., p. 159.
36. *The Hill of Dreams* (New York: Knopf, 1923), p. 47.
37. Ibid., p. 267.
38. Ibid., p. 183.
39. Ibid., p. 152.
40. Ibid., p. 197.
41. "True Comfort," *Academy and Literature*, 25 May 1912, p. 647.
42. *The Secret Glory*, pp. 147-48.
43. Cf. ibid., p. 237.
44. *The Secret Glory*, conclusion, ms., Yale University Library, pp. 356-57.
45. *Hieroglyphics*, p. 54.
46. *Tales of Horror and the Supernatural* (New York: Knopf, 1948), p. 219.
47. *Things Near and Far*, p. 175.
48. Ibid., p. 83.
49. "Introduction" to *The Hill of Dreams*, pp. xiii-xiv.
50. *Far Off Things*, p. 101.
51. *The London Adventure*, p. 142.
52. Ibid., pp. 91-93.
53. *Far Off Things*, p. 116.
54. In his notes to Henry Danielson's *Arthur Machen: A Bibliography* (London: Henry Danielson, 1923), p. 47.

Richard Middleton:
Beauty, Sadness, and Terror

Darrell Schweitzer

I

". . . he was the Bohemian personified," editor John Gawsworth wrote, "One of the 'rare' spirits in the Elizabethan, jovial
sense of that antique adjective. Simplicity—the keynote of his
art—was also the keynote of his Alsatian mode of living; for all his
learning, for all his passion, he could not 'grow up.'"

Arthur Machen praised his genius and wrote of the title story of
his principal collection, "I would not exchange this short, crazy,
enchanting fantasy for a whole wilderness of seemly novels."

Lord Alfred Douglas found him "a witty and whimsical talker."

But in 1911, Richard Barnham Middleton, the author of "The
Ghost Ship," one of the most cheerful pieces of supernatural *fun* in
English literature, killed himself in his sordid lodgings in Brussels
by drinking chloroform. He had been ill for some time, had suffered the pangs of unrequited love, and was apparently in despair
over the future of his literary career. He was twenty-nine. Machen
was writing the introduction to a memorial volume.

Middleton's friends at the time doubtless asked "Why?" Today
the same question gives his work an added, if morbid fascination,
quite aside from its very real merit. We search it for suicide notes,
as surely as we do Robert E. Howard's poetry. We find a great deal
about death, unhappiness, and despair; the answer is as simple as
all that and also more complex. That one famous story, "The Ghost
Ship," wonderful as it is, is quickly seen as amazingly atypical.

II

Richard Middleton was born at Staines, in England, on October
28, 1882. His father, an engineer, provided a stable home environ-
ment. Schooling seems to have been ordinary enough for a
middle-class boy of the period, save that Middleton, brighter and
more sensitive than his fellows, became that archetypical, suffering

34

object of cruel fun found among every group of schoolboys. These agonies are chronicled in his story, "A Drama of Youth," which is, indeed, about a superior boy put through hell by his peers, who finds it better to say home sick. So chicken pox becomes a cause for celebration.

In real life, when the pressures on him became too great, Middleton's father moved him to another school, from which, in 1899, he passed his matriculation examination for the University of London. There he studied Elementary and Additional Mathematics, English, and what was still called "Natural Philosophy." He did well, but for some reason his college career was cut short, and he became a clerk. Office work was painful drudgery, endured for six years while he read the classics and dreamed of freedom. He began to write, and joined an informal society of literary men, The New Bohemians, of which Machen was a member.

This was his chance. He made a break for freedom, resigned his job, and became a full-time literary man, without ever having, apparently, made a shilling from writing. It was the classic mistake of the would-be writer, but one which many writers have managed to survive.

His social connections did him good service. Lord Alfred Douglas (the same who, years before, had been Oscar Wilde's unindicted partner in iniquity) made him a book reviewer for *The Academy*, which he edited. Edgar Jepson made him a sub-editor of *Vanity Fair.* By 1908 he was being published fairly widely in British periodicals, although book publication eluded him. He developed a following as a poet. Austin Harrison of *The English Review* called him the "carol-boy of English poetry. . .our Verlaine."

This was at least a modest level of success. However discontented Middleton may have been, there were doubtless thousands of struggling hopefuls who never got as far as the pages of *The Century* or *Vanity Fair.* He did not make much money, but then, as now, the serious money was in novels and book-length non-fiction. Middleton's work consisted of short stories, prose sketches, essays, and poems, and while he had little difficulty placing them, it was only natural that it would take time for his reputation to grow. Book publication would have come eventually, if he had only been patient.

Of course he was not patient, and it is very easy to lecture a man long dead about how he should have run his career. Logically, Middleton should have held whatever jobs he could which would still enable him to write, then gone on that way until he was earning enough from writing that he could afford to go full-time. Perhaps he would never have made a living from writing. Many writers, even great ones, don't. All Middleton needed was a job, and his poverty and subsequent sufferings could have been avoided.

But he was no more logical than most of us. His passions and ambitions drove him, and perhaps too some deap-seated urge he did not understand. He was the living stereotype of the Romantic poet, a wildly impractical seeker-after-beauty who never manages to adjust to the prosaic world and hurts when the world fails to adjust to him. Gawsworth tells us that he even looked the part, ". . .a sturdy, broad-shouldered man with the darkest and shaggiest of black beards, his thick lower lip gleaming like a wet cherry from out its opulence. . .his pockets bulged with drafts of poems, scrawled upon old envelopes, and stories illegibly recorded on the backs of bills." Middleton did not plan his life. He lived it, and things, in time, did not work out happily.

It is not entirely clear with whom he was in love, but there were bad love affairs which depressed him, and he was already that sort of person whose emotions ran in a roller-coaster ride from wild elation to deep melancholy and back again. He wrote love poems to a prostitute, which only fits the Romantic image. Gawsworth says, "he could find in the eyes of the most degraded wanton. . .the picture of 'the best sort of fairy' and, further, celebrate this finding of purity amid defilement in flowing music." One wonders if the prostitute ever knew she was the object of such affections. The image of the Romantic Poet and the living man become difficult to separate. Perhaps Middleton couldn't do it either.

He moved to Brussels in 1911 and contined to write, mostly prose by this time, as the failed love affairs seem to have silenced his muse. His work continued to appear in various magazines, but the real world began to close in on his dream of freedom from everyday cares. He was desperately short of money. His health worsened, and he suffered increasing attacks of neuralgia. (That is, sharp pain from a variety of causes; neuralgia being one of those ailments, like dropsy, which turns out to be a miscellany of symptoms rather than a specific disease. It is even possible that in Middleton's case the pains were psycho-somatic.) He had been prescribed chloroform, and on December 1, 1911, when there seemed to be no other way out, he drank some. To the end he maintained a cheerful façade, but it was indeed only a façade. His last message to his friend Henry Savage was, "Goodbye, Harry, I'm going adventuring again."

It was a cruel irony, which he no doubt would have expected, that as soon as he was dead, Middleton was proclaimed a lost, neglected genius. Five memorial volumes appeared within two years: *The Ghost Ship and Other Stories* (his best fiction), *Monologues* (essays), *The Day Before Yesterday* (reminiscences of childhood in the manner of Barrie's *The Golden Age)*, and two volumes of poetry. More followed: a play, a collection of his letters to Henry Savage, and finally, in 1933, *The Pantomime Man*, a gathering of uncollected stories, essays, and sketches edited by Gawsworth, who had become his champion. There are further uncollected stories in Gawsworth's anthologies, no less than six in *New Tales of Horror by Eminent Authors* (1934). Vincent Starrett's *Buried Caesars* (1923) contains an essay about him, which examines, then dismisses, the idea that genius is somehow inherently self-destructive. Middleton's death, Starrett muses, "must have been, partially, in the nature of a protest. . . [his] beautiful writings were placed in covers *after* his death. . . . Suppose someone had whispered a few words of sympathy and appreciation, and it had been a bit less difficult for him to live and write and sell his tales!"

If only. Richard Middleton's life and death were a long series of if-onlys. There is a great deal about death in his work, but, as Starrett points out, there usually is in the writings of youth. Quite unlike fantasy fiction's other famous suicide, Robert E. Howard, Middleton seems to have been a basically healthy personality. There was no horrible fixation driving him inexorably to his doom. Middleton's suicide probably came as a surprise, even to Middleton. He merely failed to get past one particularly difficult stretch of living.

If only—

Middleton was still young when he died, and his talent was perhaps not fully developed, but it was already abundantly clear that the loss to literature was very great. His enormous promise had already yielded enormous accomplishments in many areas, not the least of which where his tales of the fantastic and grotesque. Starrett said that Middleton "looked out of a window and dreamed fantastic dreams."

Indeed he did, and some of them were nightmares.

III

"The Ghost Ship" is a jolly tale about a phantom galleon blown into a turnip patch in a respectable English village. In time the rowdy spectres have so upset the villagers' sense of propriety that they must leave, taking all the local ghosts with them. The once richly-haunted place is left with hardly a streamer of ectoplasm. Without a doubt this is one of the most successful humorous ghost stories of all time. It used to be a standard item in anthologies, and it deserved its fame. More remarkable, it hasn't aged at all. Humor often doesn't hold up over even a few decades.

Most of Middleton's fiction, however, is beautiful and sad. There is a pervading sense of helpless melancholy, as if he were aware that life would never conform to his beautiful notions. "The Soul of the Policeman" is about precisely this conflict. The policeman is so ready to see the good and the beautiful that he forgives criminals and can't keep up his arrest quota. "The Poet's Allegory" is more of a direct polemic, about a poet who sings of beautiful things and is ignored, then turns scurrilous and develops a large following.

About a quarter of Middleton's stories have clear fantastic elements. Many more have the "feel" of fantasy, and are right on the edge of non-reality. "Children of the Moon," for example, is about two children in search of "magic" (in the broadest sense) by moonlight. Anything they see, presumably, is only in their minds, but the point is a sad irony: only an escaped lunatic can understand their quest.

In "The Bird in the Garden," a child dwells in a fabulous garden and waits with messianic expectation for "a bird of all colors, ugly and beautiful, with a harsh sweet voice." But one day the child disastrously "awakens" into the mundane world: a sordid basement tenement with a few flowerpots hanging from a grating. This child, like many of Middleton's characters, is trapped by life. It is no one's fault. Things merely are. The boy-tramp in "On the Brighton Road" coughs out an account of his wanderings. He is very ill, perhaps dying. It turns out that he has already died many times along the road, and is condemned to repeat his death over and over. (The story makes an interesting contrast to the realistic "The Boy Errant," in which a fourteen-year-old vagabond seems happy with his lot, but his fears are briefly and poignantly revealed.) The inept magician in "The Conjurer" tempts fate in his

38

one last, desperate attempt to save his career. He succeeds in making his wife disappear, but can't get her back. There is no moral reason for this. It is a fluke of cruel, existential weirdness. Similarly, there is no explanation for the sinister activities of "The Coffin Merchant," who only gives his handbills to people who will be needing his services shortly. Middleton's world never offers an easy answer. "Shepherd's Boy" was neglected by his drunkard father and killed in a stupid accident, but his ghost still tends the sheep. Why? There is no reason.

Middleton was capable of straight-out grue. The title object of "The Hand" is found severed on a tabletop by a character groping about in the dark. "Wet Eyes and Sad Mouth" is a chilling study of the mind of a murderer as he contemplates the woman he has just strangled. In "The Luck of Keith-Martin," a traveller comes to the darkened residence of an old friend. A woman's voice bids him leave. He persists and turns on the lights, only to discover that the woman has murdered his friend and is drenched in his blood. Even more bizarre is "The Making of a Man," in which an immature wimp of a clerk comes upon a woman in need of help—she has just murdered a man and needs help choppingup the body. So he pitches in and finally "caught her in his arms and kissed his boyhood away on her hot face." More pathetic is "Who Shall Say—?," about two small children who must decide what to do, now that their father has announced that he has murdered their mother. Grue and helplessness come together to an absurd degree in "The Murderer," in which the suicidal protagonist cast himself before an oncoming train. But inexplicably, after he feels himself run over, he finds himself alive and under arrest for murder, having pushed a duplicate of himself in front of the train. His last recorded words are, "Can a man die twice?"

The boy on the Brighton road knew the answer.

IV

All this comes into focus when we remember that the author was a suicide, as if Middleton's death formed an artistically correct conclusion to his career. But his work can be appreciated without any knowledge of who the author was or how he died. At his best, Middleton was a master of form. He wrote beautiful prose, and, as in "Shepherd's Boy," he could create a vivid, dark miniature in only a few hundred words. He had an exquisite aesthetic sense, a little commoner in his generation, but rare in any. Oscar Wilde, Lord Dunsany, Walter de la Mare, and a few others shared it. More than that, Middleton wrote with conviction. The unreality shimmering right at the edge of the ostensibly realistic stories is genuine, not an affectation. Middleton saw life as an uncertain thing. Like the boy on the Brighton road, we go on and on, past all miseries, but like the child in "The Bird in the Garden," our circumstances might become much worse if we suddenly "awaken."

Arthur Machen considered Middleton to be a great artist because he understood that the universe is a "mystery." But Middleton, unlike Machen, never learned to live with the mystery.

Books by Richard Middleton:

The Ghost Ship and Other Stories (1912)
Poems and Songs, First Series (1912)
Poems and Songs, Second Series (1912)
The Day Before Yesterday (1912)
Monologues (1913)
These five were published by T. Fisher Unwin in Britain and by Michael Kennerley in the U.S.

The District Visitor (The Norman, Remington Co., 1924)
Richard Middleton's Letters to Henry Savage (The Mandrake Press, 1929)
The Pantomime Man (Rich & Cowan, 1933)

About Middleton:

Stephen Wayne Foster, "A Poet's Death: Richard Middleton," in *The Romanticist*, No. 4-5, 1982.
Henry Savage, *Richard Middleton, The Man and His Work* (Cecil Palmer, 1922).
Vincent Starrett, "Two Suicides," in *Buried Caesars* (Covici-McGee Co., 1923).

FULL FATHOM FIVE:
THE SUPERNATURAL FICTION
OF WILLIAM HOPE HODGSON

Alan Warren

You gentlemen of England
That live at home at ease,
Ah! little do you think upon
The dangers of the seas.
—Martyn Parker, *Song*

"Wouldst thou,"—so the helmsman answered,
"Learn the secret of the sea?
Only those who brave its dangers
Comprehend its mystery!"
—Longfellow, *The Secret of the Sea*

The dragon-green, the luminous,
the dark, the serpent-haunted sea.
—James Elroy Flecker, *The Gates of Damascus*, "West Gate"

Horror writers old and new have staked out certain territories for themselves: Blackwood wrote of the outdoors, of the malignity of the woods and forests; Ray Bradbury explored the joys and terrors of childhold; Robert Bloch has been described as the master of psychological horror. In the same way, William Hope Hodgson's domain is the sea. No one in the horror genre captured so well its brooding malevolence, nor has anyone returned with such frequency to its "serpent-haunted" waters.

To admit his faults at the outset: he was no stylist, and had no gift for characterization or plot. In addition, a cloying sentimentalism, a product of Hodgson's Victorian outlook, pervades much of his work. Yet, paradoxically, had he been a more learned man or a more gifted stylist his stories might be less memorable, for their very crudeness gives them a raw power, making him one of the "purest" of horror writers. He has certain affinities with W. Clark Russell, another chronicler of watery deaths and sea serpents, remembered today solely through Dr. Watson's reference in the Sherlock Holmes story "The Five Orange Pips." Yet while Russell is for-

41

gotten, Hodgson has achieved cult-status. His tenebrous horrors carry a genuine *frisson*, probably because Hodgson, in writing about the sea, was exorcising a personal demon. This gives his best stories a distinctive quality and has led to inflated comparisons with Melville and Conrad. Closer to the truth was this encomium from H.P. Lovecraft:

"Of rather uneven stylistic quality, but vast occasional power in its suggestion of lurking worlds and beings behind the ordinary surface of life, is the work of William Hope Hodgson, known today far less than it deserves to be." (From "Supernatural Horror in Literature".)

Hodgson was born on 15 November 1877, the son of an Anglican priest. At the age of thirteen he tried to run away to sea, but his family brought him back. A year later he was allowed to be apprenticed as a cabin boy in the merchant marine for four years. He completed this apprenticeship in 1895 and spent two years in school in Liverpool, where he qualified for a mate's certificate. He took up photography as a hobby, and photographed the sea during severe storms. His visual sense served him well in describing sea monsters, and he put his knowledge of photography to use in his Carnacki stories.

Slight of build, with an unimposing physique, Hodgson became an ardent student of physical fitness, primarily because he was an easy target for bullies aboard ship. He even studied judo. As Sam Moskowitz notes in his essay, "William Hope Hodgson—The Early Years," published in *Weird Tales*, "There is strong evidence that throughout his life one of his most delightful diversions was to pound seamen to jelly at the slightest provocation."

His enthusiasm for the sea palled. Some years later Hodgson published a piece in *The Grand Magazine*. In response to the question "Is the Mercantile Navy Worth Joining", Hodgson's reply was entitled "Certainly Not," and read, in part:

"I am not at sea because I object to bad treatment, poor food, poor wages, and worse prospects. I am not at sea because very early I discovered that it is a comfortless, weariful and thankless life—a life compact of hardness and sordidness such as shore people can scarcely conceive. I am not at sea because I dislike being a pawn with the sea for a board and the shipowners for players."

In 1899 Hodgson left the sea for good and opened a "School of Physical Culture" in Blackburn, a small city north of Liverpool. In

1902 Hodgson attended a performance by Harry Houdini in which the great magician claimed that he could escape from any handcuffs, chains or bonds ever made. Hodgson took up the challenge, manacling him with such force—and knowledge of muscle and sinew—that it took Houdini, bloody but unbowed, two hours to escape. Houdini, understandably bitter toward Hodgson, claimed that this had been the cruelest treatment he had ever received.

Hodgson began turning his energies to writing, first with articles about physical culture, then fiction. His first story, "The Goddess of Death," was published in 1904, and Hodgson received twenty-eight dollars for it. But it was his second story that set the seal on his career as a writer. "A Tropical Horror," published in *The Grand Magazine* in June, 1905, concerns a huge sea serpent that comes aboard a ship in the Pacific. The monster weighs at least 100 tons, has a "huge barrel-like head," a great tongue, and little pig-eyes "that seem to twinkle with a diabolical intelligence." It begins killing the crew members, leaving only the narrator.

In 1905 another market opened up for Hodgson: *The Monthly Story Magazine*.

"From the Tideless Sea," published in their April 1906 issue, is set in the mythical Sargasso sea, a dreary, dead-calm area of slime and rotting seaweed, of dead ships and gigantic Octopi. Other horror writers have used this setting, but no one has used it so consistently or described its acrid hideousness as vividly as Hodgson.

"The Mystery of the Derelict" was published in the July 1907 issue of *The Story Teller*, and marks Hodgson's second use of the Sargasso Sea mythos. This story, featuring gigantic mutated rats that feast on ten men who set out to investigate an ancient derelict, finds a distant echo in Stephen King's 1970 story "Graveyard Shift."

That same year, 1907, Hodgson published a story in *The Blue Book Magazine* that owes a debt to Conan Doyle. "The Terror of the Water Tank" deals with two men found strangled beside a large water tank. A caretaker is arrested for the murders, and is sentenced to be hanged. Dr. Tointon, a forerunner of Hodgson's psychic detective Carnacki, deduces that a ribbon-shaped creature *inside* the tank is responsible. After a tense vigil, he kills the creature. When asked what it was, he replies, "It is one of those abnormalities that occasionally astonish the scientific world. It is a creature that has developed under abnormal conditions. . . ."

Hodgson published his first novel in 1907. *The Boats of the "Glen Carrig"* is set in the Sargasso Sea, and deals with ship-wrecked sailors trapped amid gigantic crabs and monstrous beings with tentacled arms and octopus-like beaks. The sailors of the *Glen Carrig* board a ship trapped in the weeds, and after numerous horrific encounters the well-to-do narrator marries a girl born aboard the ship.

The Boats of the "Glen Carrig" is not so much a novel as a series of horrific incidents strung together by the merest pretense of plot. It has pace and a wealth of incidents but is crudely structured, as might be expected of a first novel.

"The Voice in the Night," published in the November 1907 *Blue Book Magazine,* is Hodgson's finest short story. It concerns two men on a schooner becalmed in the northern Pacific who encounter an unseen presence in the darkness—a voice, "curiously throaty and inhuman," that calls out for provisions. But when the two men raise a light the presence strenuously objects. They supply him with provisions; he rows away, then returns to tell them his story. He and his fiancée were left on board a sinking ship. They built a raft and drifted toward a large sailing vessel. The man climbed aboard, only to find the decks covered with a gray, lichenous fungus "which blotched the side of the ship lividly." His fiancée comes aboard; they find provisions, but the loathsome fungi are everywhere, "some of them rising into nodules several feet in height." When this grows unbearable they leave the ship and set up tents on an island, only to find growths of fungus on their own bodies—first in small circular spots, like moles. Soon the supply of food begins to run out, and one day the man comes back to find his fiancée eating the fungus. Late that day the man sees a distorted, vaguely human creature—one of the men who had come to the island from the ship. It detaches itself from a mass of the stuff and rubs it across his lips, and, to his horror, he himself begins to devour the fungus. As he finishes his story and begins to row himself back to the island, the sun ". . .lit up the receding boat with a gloomy fire. Indistinctly I saw something nodding between the oars. I thought of a sponge—a great, gray nodding sponge. The oars continued to ply. They were gray—as was the boat—and my eyes searched a moment vainly for the conjunction of hand and oar." *(Deep Waters,* p. 168).

If Hodgson is to be remembered for a single story, it is this one. The tense atmosphere of the opening, with the muffled sound of oars in the misty night, culminates in all-encompassing horror, yet there is also a note of pity for the brave, doomed victim and his fiancée. For once, Hodgson's sentimentality was put to good effect.*

In 1908 Hodgson published his second novel, *The House on the Borderland*. It marked a considerable advance over its predecessor, and is easily Hodgson's most visionary work. Its subtitle, designed to enhance the story's verisimilitude, reads: "From the Manuscript, discovered in 1877 by Messrs. Tonnison and Berreggnog, in the Ruins that lie to the South of the Village of Kraighten, in the West of Ireland. Set out here, with Notes by William Hope Hodgson." Hodgson's "Notes" make it clear that he is wary of interpreting the events described: "The inner story much be uncovered, personally, by each reader, according to ability and desire." (Author's Introduction)

Even with these preliminaries, the story is told within a framing device: two travelers come upon a manuscript in the fragment of a great ruin built on the edge of a chasm. The manuscript is entitled "The House on the Borderland" and its narrator warns that the peasants consider him mad. He lives with his sister and a dog in a house with a bad reputation. He experiences visions; he describes one in which he floats across "The Plain of Silence." A jade house resembling his own sits in an amphitheatre. In the mountains stand monstrous creatures. A monster resembling a swine tries to get into the house. The narrator regains consciousness, only to find that twenty-four hours have passed. His dog chases a white "thing" into a chasm, and swine creatures besiege the house. His sister lapses into a state of mental imbalance.

The narrator experiences another vision. In a passage directly inspired by H.G. Wells's *The Time Machine*, time begins to speed up. The hands of his clock spin. Time itself begins to lose definition. His dog dissolves into dust—the true corporeal state of any living thing. The sun cools; the earth is blanketed with snow. And:

"It might have been a million years later that I perceived, beyond possiblity of doubt, that the fiery sheet that lit the world, was indeed darkening.

"Another vast space went by, and the whole enormous flame had sunk to a deep, copper colour. Gradually, it darkened, from copper to copper-red, and from this, at times, to a deep, heavy, purplish tint, with, in it, a strange loom of blood.

"Although the light was decreasing, I could perceive no diminishment in the apparent speed of the sun. It still spread itself in that dazzling veil of speed.

"The world, so much of it as I could see, had assumed a dreadful shade of gloom, as though, in very deed, the last day of the world approached." (XVII, P. 106)

The earth begins traveling toward a giant green star that is the center of the universe. He returns to the Plain of Silence and finds the damage to the jade house is identical to the damage to his own.

He acquires another dog, which is attacked and wounded by the creatures outside. The wound soon takes on a fungoid appearance, and when the dog licks his hand a small scratch begins to glow in the dark. He shoots the dog, but the damage is done: the fungoid growth proceeds up his arm to his side and neck. The swine monster returns, and the narrator is left waiting for him. He hears something coming up the steps. There the manuscript ends. Berreggnog asks whether the narrator was mad. Tonnison insists he was not. A poem, entitled "Grief," is appended to the manscript.

The House on the Borderland is Hodgson's most impressive work, and his most obscure. Its metaphysical aspects impressed several critics, notably H.P. Lovecraft, who termed it "Perhaps the greatest of all Mr. Hodgson's works." Its obscurities derive from the relative lack of sophistication of its author. It is tempting to read it as the narrative of a madman, but this notion can be discarded, not only because of Tonnison's emphatic denial, but because Hodgson himself was hardly interested in aberrant psychological states. A Freudian reading is more plausible. The swine creatures are sexual, and since they represent the physical, carnal side of man, they are described as foul and loathsome. The pit from which they emerge is a clear sexual symbol:

"A little to my left, the side of the pit appeared to have collapsed altogether, forming a deep V-shaped cleft. . . ." (XI, p. 68)

Appropriately, true spiritual love is represented by the soulmate the narrator encounters while traveling through time. For Hodgson, with his Victorian sensibilities, this spiritual love was much preferable to carnality, against which man must always be on his guard. When the swine creatures emerge, appropriately, from the "bowels of the world," they bring with them death and festering decay. True immortality is attainable only through spirituality; if man concentrates only on the physical he will wind up, like the narrator's dog, a pile of dust.

Allied to this is the central theme of the book: the tyranny of time itself. The very ambitiousness of this theme was too much for its author. For all his ability at evoking fear (and indeed personifying it in the figure of the hog, a monstrous entity he would return to in his Carnacki stories), Hodgson was not the equal of H.W. Wells, and it would have required a writer of Wells's ability to suitably treat this theme. Still, as an ambitious and horripilating work, *The House on the Borderland* is probably Hodgson's most impressive novel.

The Ghost Pirates (1909) was more conventional. In a special note appended to the first edition, Hodgson stated that he considered it the third in a trilogy, along with *The Boats of the"Glen Carrig"* and *The House on the Borderland.* It is, again, a story of strange events at sea, this time on board the *Mortzestus,* out of San Francisco. This ship, described as having "too many shadows," is in fact awash in ghosts: one rises from the sea to board her, then walks back into the waves. Sailors are hauled off to death. The narrator evolves a theory that the earth is inhabited by two forms of life, one solid and the other ethereal, but as real as the first. After numerous ghostly encounters, including one in which the narrator is nearly torn loose from the rigging by some unseen force, four vessels are seen underneath the waves. Ghost pirates emerge from these ships, killing everyone aboard but the narrator. The ship is dragged down into the sea. The narrator is swept away and rescued by another ship.

The Ghost Pirates is not as ambitious as *The House on the Borderland,* nor as obscure. It presents a strong narrative, told forcefully and straightforwardly, with careful attention to mood and atmosphere. As a sustained mood piece, a full-length supernatural sea thriller, it has no peer.

In 1910 Hodgson began publishing a series of short stories about Carnacki, a psychic investigator. A hybrid of Sherlock Holmes and Algernon Blackwood's John Silence, Carnacki investigates hauntings and other supernatural occurrences, and attempts to determine their origin. If a supernatural agency is at work he employs pentagrams and metaphysical apparatus; if the agency is human he exposes the hoaxers and turns them over to the police.

Obviously envisioning an extended career for his psychic sleuth à la Conan Doyle, Hodgson erred by failing to imbue him with any shred of characterization. Carnacki is merely the hanger on which the raiments of plot are hung, sadly lacking in human qualities and possessing none of Holmes's indomitable intellectual force. The stories are further hampered by Hodgson's tendency to spoil truly frightening set-pieces by resorting to "natural" explanations, usually involving wires and mechanical devices, the operation of which would tax the showmanship abilities of Houdini. In addition, the framework of the stories—told in the first person, with Carnacki addressing his friends—is formulaic. All this admitted, the Carnacki stories occasionally rise to notable heights of terror, usually when Hodgson is sensible enough to allow the supernatural element to predominate.

"The House Among the Laurels" is typical: In an old mansion in western Ireland two tramps have died under mysterious conditions. A group of locals go to investigate. Once the investigators are inside Gannington Manor, blood begins to drip, and a dog they have brought with them lets out a mournful howl. It is later found with its neck broken. Carnacki is called in to investigate. and he brings along six constables armed with rifles. He draws a circle with chalk, smudging it with garlic, and they sit down to wait. Carnacki feels safe within his pentacle, and as he tells his friends, "It is difficult to suggest an explanation non-technically, and if you are really interested you should read Garder's Lecture on 'Astarral Vibrations Compared with Matero-involuted Vibrations below the Six-Billion Limit.'" (*Carnacki, The Ghost-Finder*, p. 67)

Despite all his precautions, the same thing happens—blood begins to drip, and a boar-hound has its neck broken. The six constables take off running, with Carnacki right behind them. He has photographed something interesting, however—a fine wire, used to open doors that seemingly unlatched themselves. He returns to the house and finds there a group of men, members of a certain "political club much wanted by the authorities." The blood was simply colored water dripped through crevices in the ceiling. The death of the two tramps remains a mystery.

This ludicrous ending leaves much to be explained, and spoils a story which until then had been proceeding admirably. Gannington Manor, with its "dismal, dripping laurels," is memorably creepy, and the seemingly supernatural menace is sharply evoked, which makes the flat denouement that much more of a disappointment.

"The Whistling Room" is probably the best of the Carnacki stories. Also set in Ireland, it concerns a room in a castle from which is heard a hellish whistling sound. Carnacki is dubious about the origins of the sound—some of the locals have taken a dislike to the castle's owner—but it turns out to be a true haunting. Carnacki positions a ladder outside the room's window and, looking in, sees:

"The floor in the middle of the huge, empty room was puckered upwards in the center into a strange, soft-looking mound parted at the top into an everchanging hole that pulsated to that great gentle hooning. At times, as I watched, I saw the heaving of the indented mound gap with a queer, inward suction as with the drawing of an enormous breath, then the thing would dilate and pout once more to the incredible melody. And suddenly as I stared, dumb, it come to me that the thing was living. I was looking at two enormous, blackened lips, blistered and brutal, there in the pale moonlight. . . ." (p. 95)

Carnacki is lured into the room by what he thinks is the cry of his friend, but it is a trap. The room's lips come toward him, and he is saved only when he hears "the unknown Last Line of the Saaamaaa Ritual" whispered in the room.

"The Whistling Room" is one of Hodgson's most bizarre and impressive feats of imagination. There are no wires or mechanical devices; the origin of the whistling room is treated seriously, and the explanation is satisfying without seeming banal.

Other Carnacki stories recall Hodgson novels. "The Haunted Jarvee" looks backward to *The Ghost Pirates* and places Carnacki aboard a haunted ship. "The Hog" recalls *The House on the Borderland*: the swinish title creature is explained in terms of astrophysics. Horror thus yields to crudely stated science fiction. These, and other Carnacki stories, suffer from Hodgson's habit of referring to such superfluous esoterica as "the Sigsand MS." and the "Aeiirii and Saiitii developments."

Six Carnacki stories were gathered into a collection, *Carnacki, The Ghost-Finder*, published in 1913. A later edition published by Mycroft and Moran in 1947 added three stories.

Hodgson published his last novel in 1912. *The Night Land* is set millions of years in the future. The sun is dead, and the remainder of humanity lives underground in a giant metal pyramid, The Great Redoubt. The hero, who works in the Pyramid, has picked up a telepathic distress call from a young woman named Naani. She lives in the Lesser Redoubt, hundreds of miles away across a land peopled by monstrous creatures. The hero's journey thus in-

.volves him with innumerable monstrosities, each more ghastly than the last, which Hodgson describes with ingenuity and imagination.

The Night Land is a quest novel told in a cumbersome, fake-archaic patois in which the dialect threatens to overwhelm all else. Large portions of it are virtually unreadable. In addition, it is over-long, and Hodgson's mawkish sentimentality is given free rein throughout. It is Hodgson's most ambitious work, and the most grievously flawed. Hodgson evidently considered it his supreme achievement, but even he must have been aware of its failings, as he cut and revised it; this version was released in America as *The Dream of X* that same year.

In 1913 Hodgson married Betty Farnsworth, and they settled in southern France. Hodgson continued to write short stories. Finding that markets for horror and science fiction were becoming limited, he wrote historical fiction, detective, humor, war, love stories and even westerns. A collection of his sea horror stories, *Men of the Deep Waters*, was published in 1914. Critics invoked the name of Poe in their mostly generous reviews. The collection, which included "The Voice in the Night," "From the Tideless Sea," and "The Derelict," did not sell well.

With the advent of World War I Hodgson and his wife returned to England. He refused sea duty and instead received a commission as a Lieutenant in the Royal Field Artillery. After a severe head injury incurred from a fall from a horse he was discharged, but soon recovered and re-enlisted. In 1917 he was sent to France; on 17 April 1918 he was killed in action near Ypres from a shell burst. His wife later had two books of his verse published in 1920 as a tribute to his memory.

Hodgson's work slipped into obscurity during the twenties, but interest revived due to the Lovecraft circle, which popularized his work. August Derleth made it available once again when he published an omnibus volume, *The House on the Borderland and Other Novels*, in 1946 under the Arkham House imprint. This was followed by *Carnacki, The Ghost-Finder*, and in 1967 Arkham House issued *Deep Waters*, a collection of his best supernatural sea stories.

Today there is more interest in Hodgson than ever before, and that interest seems to be continuing. Perhaps Lovecraft best summed up the appeal of Hodgson and his work, when he wrote in "Supernatural Horror in Literature":

"Mr. Hodgson is perhaps second only to Algernon Blackwood in his serious treatment of unreality. Few can equal him in adumbrating the nearness of nameless forces and monstrous besieging entities through casual hints and insignificant details, or in conveying feelings of the spectral and the abnormal in connection with regions and buildings."

WILLIAM HOPE HODGSON: A BIBLIOGRAPHY

The Boats of the "Glen Carrig". London: Chapman and Hall, 1907. (Reprinted by Hyperion, 1976).

The House on the Borderland. London: Chapman and Hall, 1908. (Reprinted by Ace paperbacks, 1962).

The Ghost Pirates. London: Stanley Paul, 1909. (Reprinted by Hyperion, 1977).

The Night Land. London: Everleigh Nash, 1912. (Reprinted by Ballantine paperbacks, 1972).

"Poems" and "A Dream of X." New York: R.H. Paget, 1912.

Carnacki, the Ghost Finder. London: Everleigh Nash, 1913. (Includes "The Thing Invisible," "The Gateway of the Monster," "The House Among the Laurels," "The Whistling Room," "The Searcher of the End House," "The Horse of the Invisible").

Men of the Deep Waters. London: Everleigh Nash, 1914. (Includes "The Derelict," "From the Tideless Sea," "More News from the Homebird," "The Voice in the Night," "The Mystery of the Derelict," "The Shamraken Homeward-Bounder," "Through the Vortex of a Cyclone").

Luck of the Strong. London: Everleigh Nash, 1916. (Short stories)

Captain Gault. London: Everleigh Nash, 1917. New York: MacBride, 1918. (Short stories)

The Calling of the Sea. London: Selwyn and Blount, 1920. (Poetry)

The Voice of the Ocean. London: Selwyn and Blount, 1920. (Poetry)

The House on the Borderland and Other Novels. Sauk City: Arkham House, 1946. (Includes *The Boats of the "Glen Carrig"*, *The House on the Borderland*, *The Ghost Pirates*, and *The Night Land*).

Carnacki, the Ghost Finder. Sauk City: Mycroft and Moran, 1947. London: Tom Stacey, 1972. (Includes the earlier Carnacki stories and adds "The Haunted *Jarvee*," "The Find", and "The Hog").

Deep Waters. Sauk City: Arkham House, 1967. (Includes "The Sea Horses," "The Derelict," "The Thing in the Weeds," "From the Tideless Sea," "The Island of the Ud," "The Voice in the Night," "The Adventure of the Headland," "The Mystery of the Derelict," "The *Shamraken* Homeward-Bounder," "The Stone Ship," "The Crew of the *Lancing*," "The Habitants of Middle Islet," and "The Call in the Dawn").

Out of the Storm. Providence, Rhode Island: Donald M. Grant, 1975. (Includes "A Tropical Horror," "Out of the Storm," "The Finding of the Graiken," "Eloi Eloi Lama Sabachthani," "The Terror of the Water-Tank," "The Albatross," "The Finding of the Lady Shannon").

Poems of the Sea. London: Ferret, 1977.

'The story was effectively filmed on CBS's *Suspense* during the fifties.

On the Edge: The Ghost Stories of Walter de la Mare

Gary William Crawford

Walter de la Mare (1873-1956) was one of the most respected literary figures of his day, but most of his work has fallen into obscurity. His fiction, in particular, has suffered because most of it has long been out of print. De la Mare wrote children's poetry and fiction, adult poetry, and some adult supernatural fiction. Such children's books as *The Three Mulla-Mulgars* have gained him a lasting reputation; but in this essay, we are concerned primarily with his very small body of adult ghost stories.

De la Mare was born in Charlton in Kent in England on 25 April 1873, the son of James Edward De la mare and Lucy Sophia Browning De la mare. As a young man, he worked as a bookkeeper for the British branch of the American Standard Oil Company; and he married Constance Igpen, with whom he had four children. He was granted a civil list pension in 1908 and began to write full time. He later became a publishing executive for the company Faber and Faber.

Famed scholar E. F. Bleiler has remarked that many of de la Mare's ghost stories cannot properly be categorized as supernatural fiction. This essay counters that view. For de la Mare is a master of what Peter Penzoldt has called the "inconclusive" ghost story. This is to say that de la Mare merely hints at a supernatural danger lurking on the edge of consciousness. Rarely does one find an actual ghost in de la Mare's fiction; but as Robert Aickman has said, the absence of the ghost seldom dispels the alarm.

De la Mare is, rather, concerned with another world, the world of the imagination, where one can often find the awe of beauty and terror. Thus, his stories are certainly not horror tales; instead, they are subtle, ambiguous tales with moments of heightened terror. Not only is he concerned with the other world, but he reveals a genuine concern for human beings who are caught up in the spectral.

De la Mare's novel *The Return* is the example of a story concerned with a sensitive man who finds himself changed physically into another person after falling asleep in a churchyard on the grave of a suicide. When he returns home, his family regards him as a stranger, and he cannot come to terms with the change that has occurred in him. He is thus isolated and lonely; and nearly all of de la Mare's stories emphasize loneliness and alienation.

One finds the theme of loss of identity over and over again. Even when the characters' personalities or appearances do not change, there is a struggle to find one's identity. This theme is pronounced in "Seaton's Aunt," which is regarded by some as de la Mare's masterpiece and which has been brilliantly filmed for television.

"Seaton's Aunt" is narrated from the point of view of Withers, who as a child knew Arthur Seaton at school. Seaton is a strange, reserved, boy who has few friends at school, but manages to bribe Withers with candy to come to his home in the country, where he lives with his elderly aunt. Seaton's aunt is a very bizarre woman who is obsessed with death and seems herself capable of communicating with spirits. Seaton hates his aunt, but fears her even more. Withers attempts to act as a go-between, but, he too, eventually becomes terribly frightened of her.

The second part of the story occurs when Seaton and Withers meet again as adults, and Seaton is engaged to be married. Withers learns that Seaton is still frightened of his aunt and feels that his death is imminent; but Withers tries to convince Seaton that it is all in his imagination.

Seaton eventually dies before his marriage under mysterious circumstances that are never revealed, and the suggestion is that Seaton's aunt had acted as a psychic vampire to draw the spirit out of him. Seaton, in a sense, had no identity of his own to begin with. He was in the vise-like grip of his aunt, and Withers himself can only confess that he was never really Seaton's friend at all.

In this tale, as in so many of de la Mare's others, the supernatural is merely hinted at; and they are "inconclusive" in that no explanations are ever offered. This aspect of de la Mare's fiction links him to a writer such as Henry James, who often subordinated the super-natural to the concerns of character and motivation.

Similarly, in "Out of the Deep," James returns to the house of his uncle, who has died, and he must be haunted by the ghostly memories of his childhood, before he can die peacefully because he is ill with tuberculosis. James is, like Seaton, a loner who is spiritually dead before his actual death.

In "All Hallows," a wanderer comes upon a haunted church and finds the rector has gone mad. The story is largely one of atmosphere, as the evil of the church takes on the qualities of ghostly possession for anyone who comes there. Similarly, "A Recluse" is one of de la Mare's most effective ghost stories, as a traveller becomes fascinated with the architectural details of Mr. Bloom's house. The traveller, Mr. Dash, meets Mr. Bloom and learns that he is an occultist. Eventually, Mr. Dash sees the dead corpse of Mr. Bloom, suggesting that it is merely Mr. Bloom's ghost he has known, and flees the house in terror.

These stories suggest a supernatural danger lurking on the periphery of consciousness. In fact, so many of de la Mare's stories and poems suggest the otherworldly, a supernatural realm on the very edge of perception that this must be accounted one of the major themes of his work.

In this respect, "A House" concerns Mr. Asprey, who is forced to leave the house in which he has lived all his life. He returns to it one last time and is haunted by memories of his life until he is absorbed into a fantastic world which suggests that he has died with the house. He was so linked with the house that it was part of his being.

A story such as "Crewe" reveals a servant's greed and his eventual haunting by a living scarecrow. Less directly evoking terror, "The Green Room" is about the ghost of a woman poet and a man who decides to publish her poetry. Here, as in so many of de la Mare's ghost stories, terror is often subordinate to awe. In "A. B. O.," de la Mare evokes Poe, one of his favorite authors, in a story in which a monster in a buried chest is dug up, suggesting potent evil. In "A Revenant," the ghost of Poe actually returns to haunt a lecturer in literature who has attacked Poe in one of his lectures.

The stories mentioned here are the few stories of the ghostly that de la Mare wrote. These are his adult ghost stories; but so many of his other short stories must be called children's stories and, for this reason, are not discussed here. Nevertheless, de la Mare's few contributions to spectral fiction are among the finest to appear in the first half of this century. Such writers as Robert Aickman and Ramsey Campbell, both writing after de la Mare, looked to him for inspiration, and de la Mare is pivotal figure in the evolution of the form.

Bibliography

The Connoisseur. London: William Collins, 1926. The ghost stories "All Hallows" and "Mr. Kempe" are here. But "Mr. Kempe" is not considered a supernatural tale by most scholars.

The Return. London: Edward Arnold, 1910.

The Riddle, and Other Stories. London: Selwyn and Blount, 1923.
"Seaton's Aunt," "Out of the Deep" are the only ghost stories in the volume.

On the Edge. London: Faber, 1930.
"A Recluse," "Crewe," and "The Green Room" are the only ghost stories in the book.

The Wind Blows Over. London: Faber and Faber, 1936.
"A Revenant" is the only ghost story here.

Writings About de la Mare

McCrosson, Doris Ross. *Walter de la Mare*. Boston: Twayne, 1966.

Megroz, R. L. *Walter de la Mare: A Biographical and Critical Study*. London: Hodder and Stoughton, 1924.

CHAMBERS AND *THE KING IN YELLOW*

Lee Weinstein

I

Robert William Chambers (1865-1933) was an American novelist and illustrator who was noted in his time for the large numbers of historical novels and romances he produced. The one work for which he is mainly remembered today, however, is a collection of short stories written at the beginning of his career: *The King in Yellow*.

He studied art in Paris for seven years, and returned to the United States in 1893 to begin a career as an illustrator for such magazines as *Life* and *Vogue*. The following year he had published a novel entitled *In the Quarter*, in which he wrote about his life as an artist in Paris. However, it was in 1895, when his second book was published, that he reached the turning point in his career.

This second book, *The King in Yellow*, won him so much critical acclaim that he decided to turn his career from drawing to writing. It contained, in addition to several more Parisian sketches reminiscent of *In the Quarter* and a collection of short prose poems, the five fantasy stories on which most of his fame now rests. Four of these revolved about the common theme of a fictitious evil play entitled "The King in Yellow" that had devastating effects upon its readers, and it is with these stories that we will be most concerned.

Soon after *The King in Yellow*, he had published a few more fantasy collections including *The Maker of Moons, The Mystery of Choice*, and *In Search of the Unknown*, but he was never again to equal the height of supernatural horror that he had attained at the beginning. His work quickly became commercially oriented and he turned to the production of mundane novels, which, although popular at the time, have long since been forgotten.

The King in Yellow has been referred to as the most important work in supernatural fiction between Poe and modern times, and at least one contemporary review compared the work to that of Poe. It has been reprinted many times in whole and in part, including a Books for Libraries edition in 1969, a Dover edition in 1970 (containing only the five fantasies, plus fantasies from other collections), and an Ace edition in 1964; and the individual stories have enjoyed endless reprinting in magazines and anthologies.

One of the unique aspects of the book, and probably the major reason for its popularity and influence, is the central idea of having a number of seemingly unrelated stories tied together by a common mythical background, an idea which H.P. Lovecraft was later to develop independently and much more fully. In none of the stories are we given a clear idea of what this mythical backdrop actually is, yet this gives the imagination a free rein and provides another major reason for the book's popularity. As the book review column in the June 1987 issue of *Godey's Magazine* put it, "...This group of stories, varied in idea, yet bound together by one subtile thread: the baleful influence upon the life of everyone that reads that mysterious volume, 'The King in Yellow.' The spell of this wonderful book is wisely left unexplained and vague. It floats shapelessly and stealthily into the story...like the effluvia of a fatal marsh."

E.F. Bleiler, in his introduction to the Dover edition, refers to this obscurity as "a deliberate barrier to comprehension" comparable to that in "The Mysterious Card" by Cleveland Moffett. This may be exaggerated; we are made aware of the general intent of the mythical elements, although certainly the meanings of the specific elements from the play are deliberately kept vague.

The four stories that revolve about this obscure background are "The Repairer of Reputations," "The Mask," "In the Court of the Dragon," and "The Yellow Sign." The fifth fantasy story in the book, "The Demoiselle D'Ys" is quite powerful in its own right, but is thematically unrelated to the others and will not be discussed here.

The central element of the mythos is "The King is Yellow," itself, a fictitious play in two acts, in which depravity is raised to the level of high art. The idea was apparently suggested to Chambers by *The Yellow Book*, a risque and daring periodical of the late 1890's. In a 1928 anthology of material from *The Yellow Book*, the introduction describes the periodical in terms very similar to those used by Chambers to describe his "King in Yellow." Both are "poisonous" and " sinful." An unfavorable contemporary review bearing the title "More Yellowness" also stressed the comparison of Chambers's book with the scandalous periodical, calling Chambers a "martyr to degeneracy." As Marion Zimmer Bradley pointed out in her article "The (bastard) Children of Hastur" in *Nyctalops* Num-

58

ber 6, the word "yellowness," during the late 1890's, had the connotation of wickedness, decadence, and spiritual danger. She also stressed the comparison of "The King in Yellow" with *The Yellow Book*, noting that both were credited with the ability to corrupt.

Since the first story, as we shall see, is set in the future, perhaps Chambers was extrapolating what the *Yellow Book* concept would evolve into if it were to be taken to its absurd extreme.

The stories are introduced by a poem called "Cassilda's Song." This poem, supposedly from Act 1, Scene 2 of "The King in Yellow," sets the mood by introducing us to the mysterious city of Carcosa, where black stars hang in the heavens, and twin suns rise and set. These and other related references form the mythical backdrop of the stories.

In the first story, "The Repairier of Reputations" (the stories are out of order in the Dover edition), we are introduced to the somewhat utopian atmosphere of the United States 25 years in the future. (The book was published in 1895; the story is set in 1920.) All major political problems have been solved; bigotry and intolerance have been eliminated; suicide having been legalized, the first Government Lethal Chamber has been erected. This chamber, a symbol of purification, stands in contrast to "The King in Yellow," which has "spread like an infectious disease from city to city, from continent to continent."

The plot centers around a madman named Castaigne, who, working under a deformed and insane dwarf named Wilde, hopes to become king of the United States. Castaigne, who narrates the story, tells us at the beginning that he has read "The King in Yellow" during the convalescent period following a fall from his horse. It is not made clear whether his ensuing madness is due to the injury to his head, or to his reading of the play, but it is the play that has motivated both him and Wilde in their lust for power.

"Cassilda's Song" introduced us to some of the mythical trapppings of the play. In "The Repairer of Reputations" we find that these elements, plus several new ones, are integrally related to the made lust for power that afflicts the two central characters. Thus Castaigne is pathologically fascinated by a manuscript of Wilde's, "The Imperial Dynasty of America,' which opens with the words, "When from Carcosa, the Hyades, Hastur, and Aldebaran," and ends by naming him the new king. (The significance of these and other allusions to the play will be discussed later.)

In his mad frame of reality, Castaigne believes that to become king, he must prevent his cousin Louis from marrying Constance Hawberk, Louis's fiancée. To accomplish this, Castaigne and Wilde send an assassin, another man haunted by the insidious play, to murder Constance. It is this that proves Castaigne's undoing, as foreshadowed by the assassin's self-destruction in the Government Lethal Chamber.

Yet there are strong hints that there is more to the nefarious schemes of Wilde and Castaigne than mere madness. Wilde seems to know about a secret past of Constance and her father. And he predicts correctly where a certain piece of armor, missing for years, can be found. Obviously, he does possess certain knowledge that surpasses our plane of existence. As the epigram in French at the beginning of the story warns us, "Let us not scoff at madmen; their madness will outlast ours. . . ." This possibility, that there may really be something behind their ravings, lends a certain edge of horror to their activities. Throughout the story, a deliberate ambiguity is set up regarding the reality of the narrator's delusions. In one scene, Wilde sends a Mr. Steylette from his door, who, he explains, is *the* Arnold Steylette, owner and editor-in-chief of a well-known newspaper. Wilde adds as the man leaves, "I pay him very badly, but he thinks it is a good bargain." Does Wilde actually have a powerful newspaper editor under his control? The only tangible evidence we have been given is the knock at the door, and the voice claiming to be "Mr. Steylette." Yet somehow our disbelief is partially suspended. Wilde was telling the truth about the armor.

In a following scene, Wilde goes on to say that he is in communication with ten thousand men, and that within 48 hours he can have the state and country rise *en masse* excepting places that have not received the Yellow Sign. The fanciful dream of a madman. Or is it? Where, in the smooth transition of events, did reality leave off and sheer madness begin? There lies the true horror of the piece.

Again, later in the story, Castaigne is intruded upon by his cousin Louis as he is trying on what he describes as a gold diadem studded with diamonds, which he has removed from a steel safe equipped with a time lock, in his room. This is what he will wear when he is King of America, by his "right in Hastur." Yet his cousin refers to his crown as being brass and to the safe as a "biscuit box." Perhaps the crown is brass, except in the deluded mind of Castaigne, but there is the definite possibility that Louis merely assumes it to be brass because that is the more likely possibility. And is his reference to the safe as a biscuit box to be taken literally, or as sarcasm?

In addition to these elements of psychological horror, there are a few elements of real physical horror. The description of Wilde, with his flat, pointed head, his artificial ears, and his fingerless left hand is quite gruesome. Even more horrifying are the scenes in which he has been clawed to a bloody mess by the cat he perpetually teases, and in which he finally has his throat torn open by the creature. Chambers seems to associate cats with death, as can be seen in "The Street of the Four Winds," also from *The King in Yellow,* and in "The Man at the Next Table" from *The Maker of Moons.*

From greed and lust for power, Chambers leads us to falsity and self-deceit in the second story, "The Mask." In "The Mask" we have a love story about artists in which the mythical "King in Yellow" elements fall into the background, while a science-fantasy element enters the forefront in the form of a liquid that turns living things to stone. Yet it is obvious that this story is taking place in the same *milieu* as the first one. The sculpture of "The Fates" upon which Boris Yvain is working throughout is the same sculpture that is seen standing before the Government Lethal Chamber in "The Repairer of Reputations."

The story centers on the triangular love affair between Boris, the girl Genevieve, and the protagonist, Alec. Genevieve has professed her love for Boris, and Alec has withdrawn himself until, at the turning point, he discovers that she really loves him.

The horror in this piece is much more subtle than in the previous story, and works along two parallel tracks. The first track is built around Boris's chemical solution, and the horror gradually mounts as Boris progressively petrifies a lily, a goldfish, and a rabbit; the final outcome being the accidental petrifaction of Genevieve. The second track is based on horror of a more spiritual nature, as Alec gradually comes to realize the deceptions of Genevieve and himself.

"The King in Yellow" which Alec chances upon at the turning point, seems to reflect symbolically his own condition as he falls ill. The quotation at the beginning of the story (incidentally, the only quotation from the play besides "Cassilda's Song") illustrates this symbolic connection. In the quotation, Cassilda and Camilla are terrified to find that a stranger, whom they have asked to unmask, is wearing none. This seems to be reflected at the story's turning point, when Alec realizes that he has been wearing a mask of self-deception to hide his love for Genevieve from himself, as well as from her and Boris, and that this self-deception has become an inseparable part of him. When Alec's friend, Jack Scott, asks the doctor, "What ails Alec—to wear a face like that?" as Alec succumbs to delirium, we know it is because of the two years of hiding the truth from himself and his friends. When Alec overhears the question, he immediately thinks of the Pallid Mask from the play. Assuming this to be the mask referred to in the opening quotation, it would seem that Alec has realized he is a personification of the stranger whose apparent mask is a part of him.

Again, in this story, we find the same type of ambiguity that was a keynote in "The Repairer of Reputations." When Boris calls Alec to come see the goldfish turned to stone in the magical fluid, there is "a feverish excitement in his voice." In the next sentence, Alec states, "a dull weight of fever lay on my limbs. . . ." It is shortly thereafter that he reads "The King in Yellow." Then, after Genevieve, who at this point actually is delirious with fever, reveals her love for Alec in front of Boris, Alec himself falls ill with fever and delirium. It is unclear what has caused his illness. Was his mention of "dull weight of fever" to be taken literally, or was it a reference to the "feverish excitement" in Boris's voice in the previous sentence? If we are to believe the latter, are we to assume it was the reading of the play that induced his fever? The play seems to have this sort of effect on characters in other stories. Or did he merely catch the fever from Genevieve, who also seems to have been stricken inexplicably? Here, too, her illness seems to be a symbolic externalization of her own hidden feelings. It was apparently triggered by a sprained ankle she sustained after Alec startled her, as she was crying alone.

However, the ambiguity here does not add so much to the effect of the piece as the subtle blend of beauty and horror surrounding Boris's solution. The description of the beautiful play of colors during the transformation of lilies and goldfish into their exquisitely sculpted and tinted marble counterparts, perfectly counterpoints the disgust Alec feels at the thought of turning living things to stone. The beauty overtakes the horror at the end when the effects wear off, and Alec and Genevieve, masks removed, are free to begin anew.

In the third story, "In the Court of the Dragon," we finally lose the ambiguity of the sort used in the previous tales, and come into a direct confrontation with the realm of "The King in Yellow."

The story is short, direct, and achieves considerable effect as the protagonist is pursued through the city by the pale-faced, black-garbed organist, only to awaken at the last instant before capture to confront the King in Yellow himself.

For the first time, in this story, we see the actual effect of reading the play, without the vagueness of before. We are told by the narrator at the outset that he is in the church for healing after having "three nights of physical suffering and mental trouble" from reading the play.

Throughout the course of the story, we see two frames of reality superimposed on one another: the realm of "The King in Yellow" lurking beneath the apparent reality of the Parisian streets. As the protagonist sits in the church at the beginning, he thinks he sees the organist leave twice. This duality is reasserted at the end of the chase as he awakens and thinks,

"I had slept through the sermon. . . Had I slept through the sermon?" and again with "I had escaped him. . . Had I escaped him?"

This dualism makes the story ambiguous, but on a higher level than we have seen so far. While in "The Repairer of Reputations" we were merely uncertain as to the reality of the protagonist's schemes in a concrete setting, here we are uncertain as to the concreteness of the story as a whole, presented, as it is, as an internal fantasy. The King In Yellow has become real, but only in an unreal, or at least uncertain, setting. The hints of concrete reality, the indifference of the congregation to the organist's wild playing, and the race through the streets of Paris are later negated as they are revealed to be parts of a possible dream sequence.

In "The Mask" there were hints of the nature of "The King in Yellow." In Alec's delirium of imagery from the play, the only sane thought that persisted was his own internal lie, persisting through the maddening ultimate truth of the play. "In the Court of the Dragon" now allows the nature of the play to emerge more fully. H.P. Lovecraft, in his essay "Supernatural Horror in Literature", refers to "primordial Carcosa. . .some nightmare memory of which seems to lurk latent and ominous at the back of all men's minds," and calls it an "eldritch land of primal memory." "In the Court of the Dragon" bears out this interpretation beautifully. The protagonist, after awakening in the church, realizes that he has always known who his pursuer really is. The primal memory has been awakened. He states (twice, significantly) "Death and the awful abode of lost souls, whither my weakness long ago had sent him, had changed him for every other eye but mine." It is significant that it was his *weakness* that had banished his strange pursuer. At the close the protagonist has gained the strength to realize the nature of these latent memories and to comprehend the ultimate Truth. It is only then that the church walls dissolve away to reveal the black stars and the towers of Carcosa in a dazzling example of the imagery that was Chambers's forté. Yet this is only the prelude to the final image as he sinks into the increasing waves of radiance and hears the King in Yellow whisper, "It is a fearful thing to fall into the hands of the living God!"

Thus we see that this play, the ultimate in "yellowness," is the key to unlock some unthinkably evil truth that we have long sought to suppress with decency and morality.

"The Yellow Sign" is the final story in the series, and is generally conceded to be the most powerful. Certainly it has been the most frequently anthologized, probably due to its final combination of supernatural and spiritual horror with physical horror.

We have again returned to the real setting of "The Repairer of Reputations" and "The Mask," as the protagonist, Mr. Scott, tells us when he says of the play: "If I ever had had any curiosity to read it, the awful tragedy of young Castaigne, whom I knew, prevented me. . . ." Yet the reality of the realm of "The King in Yellow," made apparent in the dream-like setting of "In the Court of the Dragon," assumes tangibility in the concrete reality shared by the first two stories. There is no denying the common dreams shared by Scott and his model, Tessie. But the corpse-like watchman, and his fight with the newsboy, remove any doubt that supernatural events are occurring. A man whose fingers come off from his soft mushy fist is not a being of the natural world. Yet it is not until the story's climax that these events begin to tie in with the play. Scott and Tessie realize that the dreams are centered around a black onyx talisman, engraved with what they discover to be the Yellow Sign, when a copy of the play mysteriously turns up in his studio. It is then that they realize the watchman has come for his talisman, but it is too late; their doom has been sealed as prophesied in the dreams.

The fantasy elements in the story closely parallel the realistic ones. The first warnings of the supernatural are Tessie's dreams of Scott being driven in a hearse by the watchman. It is a direct result of these dreams that Tessie and Scott become romantically involved with each other. This culminates in Tessie's giving of the talisman to Scott as a token of her affection, thus sealing their fate. In their whole relationship there is a hint of sin—of "yellowness." Scott feels himself unworthy of Tessie and is distraught that he has kissed her. As a result of this "sin" she is no longer able to pose nude for him; they have tasted the forbidden fruit. This anticipates her sampling the forbidden fruit of the play, resulting in his reading of it also, and their final departure from this life. But as the verse at the beginning of the story says: "Let the red dawn surmise/What we shall do/When this blue starlight dies/And all is through." With every death is the promise of rebirth. (In some reprinted versions, this verse does not appear.)

The mysterious Yellow Sign, about which the story revolves, is really the only tangible symbol of the play's content we are ever given. In "The Repairer of Reputations," the only other story that mentions it, we are given a few clues to its significance. At one point, Wilde tells Castaigne that the portions of the country that do not follow when the revolution occurs "Might better never have been inhabited," for he would not send them the Yellow Sign. Thus we see that the Yellow Sign is intended as a tangible symbol of the other reality of the play, used in this first story to indicate allegiance to the King in Yellow.

In "The Yellow Sign" we see the effect of this unasked-for sign of allegiance on two unsuspecting people. They are gradually drawn into something they are at first unaware of, and later do not understand, until finally they have read the play. It is only then that the final revelation occurs. After they have read it, Scott tells us: "I knew that she knew and read my thoughts as I read hers, for we had understood the mystery of the Hyades, and the Phantom of Truth was laid." This last remark could be interpreted as saying that the thin veil of what we consider to be truth has been torn away.

Later, after the watchman has come for his talisman and Scott lies dying, he goes on to say: "I could tell more, but I cannot see what help it would be to the world. . . . They of the outside world may send their creatures into wrecked homes and death-smitten firesides. . . but with me their spies must halt at the confessional." His reference to writers and reporters as "those of the outside world" is an important clue here. The implication is that the great Truth he has unwittingly discovered is internal. This rings true in all four of the stories. Castaigne and Wilde were dealing with what appeared to be their own mad fantasies; Alec's realization of his self-deception was, of course, internal, as was the protagonist's plight in "In the Court of the Dragon." And now here, in "The Yellow Sign," we are told, despite the physical presence of the dead watchman, that again the ultimate revelation belongs to a subjective reality. Indeed, there is no physical reason for their deaths.

II

It is well known that Chambers got much of the mythical backdrop for his imaginary play from Ambrose Bierce. Two of Bierce's minor short stories provided him with material: "Haita the Shepherd" and "An Inhabitant of Carcosa."

"Haita the Shepherd" is a parable about a young shepherd boy and his fleeting moments with a beautiful and elusive girl named Happiness. In it we see him praying to the god of the shepherds: a nondescript divinity named Hastur. This is the first appearance of a name that was to survive, in a variety of incarnations, to present-day fantasy.

"An Inhabitant of Carcosa" is a short tale about a man who has been somehow resurrected as a spirit upon the ruins of Carcosa, the ancient city that had been his home during life. The story is introduced by a short quotation describing various types of death, ascribed to someone named Hali. (Another Bierce tale, "The Death of Halpin Frayser," also begins with a quotation from this fictitious personage." The story contains a reference to Aldebaran and the Hyades, and the spirit to whom the tale itself is ascribed is named Hoseib Alar Robardin (from which Chambers borrowed the Alar).

Although it has been said that Chambers built his "King in Yellow" mythology upon the background provided by Bierce, this is not really the case. True, he borrowed names from Bierce's tales, but the use he made of them corresponds in no way to that of the original. Carcosa was no longer an ancient city of the Middle East, but a strange and fabulous place under a double sun, whose towers can be seen rising behind the moon, and where black stars hang in the heavens. Hali no longer referred to an author of mystical quotations about death, but rather to a lake whose waves are of cloud rather than water.

In "An Inhabitant of Carcosa," toward the end of the story the narrator exclaims, "Looking upward, I saw through a sudden rift in the clouds Aldebaran and the Hyades!" He has just discovered that although it appears daylight to him, it is actually night, for the stars are visible. Compare this with a line from "The Mask" in which Alec describes his fevered delirium: "Aldebaran, The Hyades, Alar, Hastur, glides through the cloud rifts which fluttered and flapped as they passed like scalloped tatters of The King in Yellow." The similarity is obvious, yet equally obvious is the change in meaning, import, and purpose that Chambers has brought about.

Special mention should be made of Chambers's use of the name Hastur, to clarify its later incorporation into the Cthulhu Mythos. Although Bierce used it as the name of a benign shepherd god, Chambers merely sprinkled the name through his stories without ever explaining what it referred to. There are a few vague clues in "The Repairer of Reputations." Castaigne says at one point, ". . .the people should know the son of Hastur," and later he raves, "I was King, King by my right in Hastur." One other grammatically ambiguous sentence mentions ". . .the establishment of the Dynasty in Carcosa, the lakes which connected Hastur, Aldebaran, and the mystery of the Hyades." Aside from these three vague references, the name Hastur, like the name Alar, only appears in groups of other names, some referring to places and some referring to people. Apparently Chambers liked the sound of the name and merely threw it in where he thought it sounded good; he didn't have any particular meaning in mind. To illustrate this, the volume's fifth fantasy story, "The Demoiselle D'Ys," although unconnected to the four King in Yellow stories, has a human character named Hastur. In his later works *The Maker of Moons* and *The Mystery of Choice*, he also plays around with names and meaningless words, carrying them from one story to another.

To the names he took from Bierce he added a large measure of his own. In additon to the Yellow Sign, and the King in Yellow himself, there are the Pallid Mask, the Phantom of Truth, Cassilda, Camilla, Demhe, Uoht, Naotalba, Aldones, and others. Some of these apparently have some import, as we have seen, while others seem to be meaningless. Cassilda and Camilla, as well as the King himself, are characters from the play, while Uoht, Thale, Naotalba and Aldones may or may not be. Demhe, like Hali, seems to refer to a lake. The Pallid Mask acts as a symbol of falsity in "The Mask," while in "The Repairer of Reputations" it seems to represent the truth of the play (". . . The State, the whole land were ready to rise and tremble before the Pallid Mask"). The Phantom of Truth seems to be a member of the Dynasty in "The Repairer of Reputations" (". . . the ramifications of the Imperial family, to Uoht and Thale, from Naotalba and Phantom of Truth, to Aldones. . . ."), while in "The Yellow Sign" the meaning, notwithstanding my earlier attempt at interpretation, is quite obscure (". . . we had understood the mystery of the Hyades and the Phantom of Truth was laid.")

It seems likely that Chambers did not have any coherent mythical structure in mind, and no concrete concept of what constituted the play, aside from the generalities touched upon. Like an impressionistic painting, it looks fine from a distance but falls apart under close scrutiny.

Marion Zimmer Bradley makes some interesting observations about the possible origins of the "King in Yellow" mythology in her article ". . . And Strange Sounding Names" in *The Conan Swordbook* (Mirage Press, 1969). She says that Chambers was influenced by a new school of impressionistic writing common at that time in France and Spain, and that most of the stories in *The King in Yellow* can be translated stylistically into Spanish without shifting a word, while the idioms are French. She theorizes, then, that Chambers, intentionally or otherwise, used names in the stories relating to the "ghosts of the Pyrenees, the endless war between Moorish pagan and sternly tenacious Spain." Thus, Mrs. Bradley concludes that Casilda [sic] is a common name among Spanish women; Hastur is a probable corruption of Asturias (a Spanish province that never surrendered to the Moors); Carcosa is a corruption of Carcasonne (an ancient French city formerly called Carcaso); and Hali is Arabic (Moorish influence on Spain) for the constellation of Taurus (which contains Aldebaran and the Hyades).

What Mrs. Bradley fails to note in her article is that with the exception of 'Casilda,' all of the aforementioned names were taken from Bierce. However, Bierce was contemporary with Chambers, and may himself have been subjected to Spanish influence.

After *The King in Yellow* Chambers never did anything to further the mythology. There are only a few small hints in his later works of its existence. In "The Silent Land," a borderline fantasy story in *The Maker of Moons*, there are two passing references to "a king in Carcosa," presented in snatches of a tale one of the characters is telling another. In *The Slayer of Souls*, a supernatural spy thriller written in 1920 (the year in which "The Repairer of Reputations" is set), we are confronted with disembodied souls indistinguishable from flesh and blood people, as in "In the Court of the Dragon." To make the point more obvious, Chambers worked into the dialogue of the novel the phrase, "It is a fearful thing to fall into the hands of the living God," the last line of "In the Court of the Dragon." There is also some background borrowed from "The Maker of Moons," which E.F. Bleiler considers to have been a preliminary version of the novel.

The real longevity of the King in Yellow mythology was due to its incorporation by other fantasy writers, long after Chambers had dropped the idea. H.P. Lovecraft was the first of these. It is often thought, in fact, that he got his idea for the *Necronomicon* from *The King in Yellow*. This, however, is not the case. The fact is that Lovecraft's first mention of the *Necronomicon* was in "The Hound," written in 1922. He did not discover the existence of *The King in Yellow* until 1927 (as is recorded in his letters) when he was finishing up his "Supernatural Horror in Literature." Moreover, there is really little resemblance between the two fictitious volumes. "The King in Yellow" is a futuristic play of such depraved beauty that it drives people mad. *The Necronomicon* is an ancient book of forbidden rites and rituals, and no one in a Lovecraft story ever went crazy from reading it.

But though he was not so obviously influenced by it, Lovecraft did revive interest in Chamber's work. He praised *The King in Yellow* in his "Supernatural Horror in Literature" (although I see no justification for his statement that the Yellow Sign was "handed down from the accursed cult of Hastur. . . ." Chambers tells of no such cult.) He also incorporated some of Chambers's mythical names in his story "The Whisperer in the Darkness" (1930). It is the only story in which he did so. Like Chambers, he did not attach any particular meaning to the names he borrowed, but merely included them in a hodge-podge of other Cthulhu Mythos names. Thus, in the story, the protagonist tells us that he found himself faced with names and terms he "had heard elsewhere in the most hideous of connections—Yuggoth. . . Azathoth, Hastur, Yian, Leng, the Lake of Hali, Bethmoora, the Yellow Sign. . . ." Later in the story we are told in a letter to the protagonist from his friend who has become involved with alien beings from Yuggoth. ". . . they [the beings from Yuggoth] have never knowingly harmed men. . . . There is a whole secret cult of evil men (a man of your mystical erudition will understand me when I link them with Hastur and the Yellow Sign) devoted to the purpose of tracking them down and injuring them on behalf of monstrous powers from other dimensions." It is obvious from the context of the story that the beings from Yuggoth are sinister creatures in league with the rest of Lovecraft's Cthulhoid pantheon. Since the second quotation turns out to be from one of the creatures, it is unclear whether it is true that they are at odds with the cults linked with Hastur and the Yellow Sign.

It was apparently this tangential reference to Hastur, however, that inspired August Derleth, Lovecraft's associate, to incorporate it into the Mythos as a relatively benign Great Old One constantly at battle with the rest of Lovecraft's pantheon. In 1932 Derleth, in collaboration with Mark Shorer, wrote "The Lair of the Star Spawn." It is in this tale that Hastur makes its first appearance as a definable entity in the Mythos. We are told that "Hastur the Unspeakable" is an evil being in league with Cthulhu *et al*. When these beings were banished by the Elder Gods, Cthulhu was inprisoned in the sunken city of R'lyeh, and Hastur was "exiled to Hali in the Hyades." In 1939 Derleth further expanded the idea in "The Return of Hastur." Here we find that Hastur is the half-brother of Cthulhu. The story tells us that "Hastur was hurled into outer space—into that place where the black stars hang, which is indicated as Aldebaran of the Hyades, which is the place mentioned by Chambers, even as he repeats the Carcosa of Bierce." Derleth also throws in a few passing references to Aldones and Thale along the way, undoubtedly to help tie together the two mythologies.

Derleth was not the only one to take a liking to the name Hastur. Marion Zimmer Bradley, herself a Chambers fan, created her own concept of Hastur, unaware of what Derleth had been doing. In 1961 *The Sword of Aldones*, the first of her Darkover novels, appeared, having as its hero a young man by the name of Regis Hastur. His family, the Hasturs, were "members of a ruling caste of telepathic families. . .ethical, serious, (and) virtuous," as Mrs. Bradley herself puts it in her article in *Nyctalops* (Number 6).

In *The Spawn of Cthulhu* (Ballantine Books, 1971) Lin Carter dredged up another example of Chambers's influence, from a 1938 issue of *Weird Tales*.

It is a short poem by the journalist Vincent Starrett, entitled "Cordelia's Song (from The King in Yellow)." It is not a bad poem, and has an eerie atmosphere about it, but aside from the title there seems to be no connection to *The King in Yellow*. In the same volume, however, Carter himself has written a sonnet sequence emulating Lovecraft's "Fungi from Yuggoth," entitled "Litany to Hastur." Carter was quite adept at imitating the styles of others, and in this sonnet sequence he achieved a subtly brilliant blend of ideas and images from Chambers, Lovecraft, and Derleth—in an atmosphere of unworldly horror.

The influence of *The King in Yellow* lives on. In 1967 Robert Silverberg opened his science fiction novel *Thorns* with the quotation from the beginning of "The Mask." And in 1973 Manly Wade Wellman's collection, *Worse Things Waiting*, was published by a new specialty press called, simply, Carcosa. Its colophon shows a weird skyline in front of the moon. The ultimate in tributes to Chambers, however, must be conceded to James Blish. His short story "More Light" in Anne McCaffrey's anthology *Alchemy and Academe* (Doubleday, 1970) is a framework in which he presents us with the entire play "The King in Yellow" as supposedly written by Chambers himself. Allegedly, Chambers actually wrote the play he had hinted at in his stories and had sent a copy to Lovecraft, who in turn sent a copy to a young fan named Bill Atheling (Blish's pseudonym). The gist of the story is that for some mysterious reasons, no one can read the entire play through.

The Blish version of the play is quite clever, and manages to include a good bit from Chambers's stories, though it does fall short on a few important points. What we are presented with is a story of a pair of stagnating cities in the midst of an interminable siege. They are the cities of Hastur and Alar, lying on the banks of the lakes Hali and Dehme [sic], respectively. With the exception of Carcosa, they are the only cities in Gondwanaland (the theoretical land mass that broke apart to form our present continents). Carcosa is a strange ghostly city that seems to float by the far shore of Hali; it is the home of the King in Yellow. Into Hastur comes a strange figure in a pallid mask and wearing the Yellow Sign; he is Yhtill, the Phantom of Truth. He entices Cassilda, queen of Hastur, to end the siege by having the entire kingdom attend a masque, all wearing a pallid mask to hide themselves from the King. The King retaliates by disintegrating Yhtill and permanently fixing the masks upon the faces of the people. The last lines echo Chambers in "The Mask": "Not upon us, Oh King, not upon us," which Alec remembers Cassilda crying, in his delirium.

71

Although he includes many such references and allusions throughout the body of the play, Blish seems to have overlooked the most obvious ones. "Cassilda's Song" and the opening quotation from "The Mask" are both cited by Chambers as being from Act 1, Scene 2 of the play, but Blish includes both in Act 2 of his version. And he totally disregards the line in "The Repairer of Reputations" that tells us of "Camilla's agonized scream and the awful words echoing through the dim streets of Carcosa. . . the last lines in the first act. . . ." No such thing happens at the end of Blish's first act, or anywhere else, for Chambers has made it plain in this line that the play is set in Carcosa, not Hastur.

However, it is all in good fun. Blish has even managed to include the Walt Whitman quotation Chambers used at the beginning of "The Maker of Moons." And of course when the King himself appears, he advises the people of Hastur, "It is a fearful thing to fall into the hands of the Living God!"

We have now had a close look at *The King in Yellow* itself, traced it origins, and followed its varied influences to the present day. No doubt even if Chambers himself is someday forgotten, Hastur will be around in one form of another to haunt the pages of fantasy.

H. Russell Wakefield:
The Man Who Believed in Ghosts

Ben P. Indick

There is a gulf between Supernatural and Horror fiction; it is sometimes bridged, but the entities nevertheless remain unique. In today's world, where power and violence appear to have overcome taste and subtlety, the Supernatural *per se* is in eclipse. Its sister, Horror, albeit in the form of *guignol*, reigns. Occasionally a contemporary master, such as Stephen King, will attempt to rediscover the method of the old school, as in his short story, "The Breathing Method," from *Different Seasons*, but the result is somewhat self-conscious. To rediscover the genre in its clearest form, one must return to the classic British school—ghostly horror tales, characterized by elegant prose, sophisticated characterization and detachment, even a remoteness, of authorial presence and temperament. These are tales less dependent upon repugnancy, which might yet produce as scarifying a climax as readers demand in our own less easily-shocked time.

It was in the fading nineteenth century and early twentieth that the supernatural story reached its apogee. The mechanisms of past gothicists, such as ancient manors, visitations from the vengeful dead, and romanticized weather conditions as a mirror of emotion remained, but in a more sophisticated and subtle style. These were the spectral tales of such great weirdistes as the inimitable M.R. James, E.F. Benson, and J.S. Le Fanu, as well as the horror tales of Bram Stoker, Algernon Blackwood and all those wonderful others who have kept our midnight hours frighteningly and deliciously shudder-filled.

Less celebrated perhaps, but no less skilful in his own manner was H. Russell Wakefield. He has left half a dozen books of spectral tales, still very effective, if less overwrought than our contempoary masters of the sinister in raising hackles. John Betjeman considered him, together with Le Fanu and Henry James, as "equal seconds" behind M.R. James as master of ghost story writing.[1] However, if Wakefield commenced his career in the manner of his idol, M.R. James, and these other masters, at the end the supernatural—for Wakefield—had become a bridgepath to horror and the grotesque.

H(erbert) Russell Wakefield was born May 9, 1888, in Kent, England, received a degree in history at Oxford University, and spent his life variously as a publisher, civil servant, and full-time writer. He died August 2, 1965. His writings include mysteries and studies of true crime as well as supernatural fiction, the last being his most important contribution. Although there is something of himself in many of his stories, the supernatural was likely of greatest personal significance to him, and is well exemplified in his very earliest work.

"The Red Lodge," his first story, is a full prototype, already displaying the format for his style: simple, direct, a tale of a house haunted by ghosts. The rationale Wakefield supplies may be vague, not fully perceived, even hearsay; ghostly personages are generally not exploited as such. Nor does he labor to obtain Samuel Taylor Coleridge's famous "suspension of disbelief"; his other-worldly persons or places are simply facts, to be accepted as such. It is by their effects upon his protagonists that these dim revenants are felt. Because it is characteristic of his methods, this story will be examined in some detail, as will examples from each of his books and periods.

Wakefield claimed to have had psychic experiences himself and apparently he did have an unpleasant psychic experience in just such a house as this lodge as a young man. Writing in 1946, he stated: "Unless I believed there *are* inexplicable phenomena in the world, marshalled under the generic term 'psychic,' I should never have bothered to write a single ghost story. . . . Actually I am convinced there are perfectly authenticated cases of most versatile psychic phenomena, for the very good reason that I have experienced them myself."[2]

In the story, a family rents the "Lodge" as a good buy, useful for their needs as well as being a "magnificent specimen of the medium-sized Queen Anne house." A neighbor, Sir William Powse, welcomes their courtesy visit but is rather circumspect about the house, urging them, with some emphasis on his words, to see him if they find it necessary. Strange and all too quickly terrifying events occur, although rarely of particularly overt supernatural nature: slime mold patches appear on the rugs without reasonable cause; a sensation of being watched is felt; the hint of a face is seen; a sound is heard—not stereotyped chains, but rather a light cough from a space behind the father, while he is reading, where he knows no one is. The images become stronger, invading dreams as well as reality.

74

Soon the spots of slime have become pools of the stuff, and the unseen antagonists are becoming more frightening. One evening the father feels himself being willed to look, in the dark of night, through the blinds, when "I knew. . .that if I did so, we were doomed." What he might have seen is not indicated, but the sense of fear is potent.

Finally they speak to Sir William, who tells them some of the dreadful events associated with the lodge in the past, even cases of death where prior renters were discovered in obvious states of terror. It is not, however, his property, and he is powerless to stop its owner from renting it. All he knows of its past in terms of a preternatural cause is a tradition dating back several centuries—when its second owner had bribed his servants to frighten his wife to death. Whatever they did, one day before dawn she ran to the river and drowned herself. Her various female successors did likewise and at length so did the husband. Sir William urges them to leave. It is difficult, even now, to accept an explanation which borders so on the incredible, and, in any event, the father regrets the loss of his three-month rental deposit. If they have had any hesitation, however, it is dispelled in a final terrifying scene when, to get out of the feared house, they are attempting to enjoy some picnicking. The sky has grown gray. Rain commences; thunder sounds. As the father and his son, the latter just recovering from fear-induced illness, begin to run back to the door into the garden, the man trips. The boy runs on and then his father sees "something slip through the door. It was green, thin, tall. It seemed to glance back at me, and what should have been its face was a patch of soused slime." Seeing it, the boy screams, and runs toward the river, the figure following him. It hovers over the boy, who flings himself into the brackish water. The father, "passing through a green and stenching film," dives after him and pulls him out of the reeds. There is no hesitation any longer. They pack and leave. But, even "as I took hold of the knob I felt a quick and powerful pressure from the other side, and it shut with a crash. The Permanent Occupants of the Red Lodge were in sole possession once more."

The economy of words and the lean, taut narration give the reader no pause, and the vagueness of the horrors allow the imagination to fill in such details as it wishes. The charm of subtlety, of suggestion and then revelation is a technique no less terrifying ultimately than that of a King, Barker or a Herbert, but the telling of it is restrained. It is less a tale of horror and repulsion, so characteristic of these later masters, than of fear and terror. H.P. Lovecraft, sensing this, wrote of Wakefield's first two collections that he "manages now and then to achieve great heights of horror despite a vitiating air of sophistication."[3]

Wakefield, however, describes his efforts and style succinctly, if good-naturedly: "Have a glance inside this book at your leisure, and then defy my hardest efforts to bring upon you the odd, insinuating little sensation that a number of small creatures are simultaneously camping on your scalp and sprinkling ice-water down your back-bone."[4]

In comparison with such a classic and contemporary master as M.R. James, Wakefield is as urbane but less light-hearted, more detached, although more likely to have lethal effects than James. Thus, in such works as "The Mezzotint," "Casting the Runes," and "Oh Whistle, and I'll Come to You, My Lad," James' interest is in the ghostly effect (which may indeed, be less than pleasant) rather than the fate of the observer or victim. Of James, Wakefield writes that he "was the last of the great ones; he closed an epoch." However, James, reviewing one of Wakefield's collections, suggested that "the author of ghost stories need not be a very violent believer himself." Wakefield denies this, and comments that James, before writing "Oh, Whistle," was "also casting a furtive inner eye at spectral heaped bed-clothes forming into fearful shapes. No doubt he soon laughed the image away, but he must have known it for a time." He concludes that "before you can scare others, you must be scared yourself."[5]

"The Red Lodge" appears in Wakefield's first book, *They Return at Evening / A Book of Ghost Stories*, published in 1928, perhaps his best collection and certainly his most definitive of the classic British ghost story.

"He Cometh and He Passeth By" surely fulfulls this description. It is forthright, firm narrative, and a good example of the basic difference in approach between Wakefield and the older, genially antiquarian-minded James. While it owes some debt to James' "Casting the Runes," it is entirely effective in its own right. It takes the existence of Evil as a given possiblity, that an individual may quite simply be evil and utilize a knowledge of Evil and Black Magic. Clichés about Far Eastern mysteries do not negate the powerful image of an Aleister Crowley-like villain, one Oscar Clinton. He has caused the death of a friend of the narrator, Bellamy. The six words which are the title of the story, scribbled on a piece of paper and recited while held against one's forehead, bring forth an unseen monstrous presence which is the mechanism of the death. In the end, it will rebound against the murderer himself.

The final paragraph is characteristic of Wakefield's style and his strength, creating a potent, lasting image while offering little in concrete description: "As Bellamy moved towards the door the lights went dim, in from the window poured a burning wind, and then from the wall in the corner a shadow began to grow. When he saw it, swift icy ripples poured through him. It grew and grew, and began to lean down towards the figure on the floor. As Bellamy took a last look back it was just touching it. He shuddered, opened the door, closed it quickly, and ran down the stairs and out into the night."

There is, for the fancier of spectral tales, a delectable taste about his understated writing. It is as though the reader was with Bellamy, *was* Bellamy, and has undergone his experience and his bitter triumph. And bitter it is, since the author writes elsewhere: "I firmly believe all such psychic intrusions possess negative survival value and should in no way be encouraged."[6]

Wakefield, in common with most British writers of his era, certainly with James, can enjoy ironic humor, even in a ghostly tale. "Professor Pownall's Oversight" is an amusing example, and a superb little tale. The professor of the title has achieved some position in life, but, for no good reason, he seems doomed always to be second to Hubert Morrison. Pownall's abiding love is chess, and it is here at least that he hopes to overcome his gnawing inferiority. He and Morrison enter the British Championship match and Morrison stays with him. The match, with the two against each other in the last round, is progressing well for Pownall, until he sees Morrison's smile of superiority. Pownall's game begins to slip, and before it is adjourned he knows he is deeply in trouble. Only a miracle can save him. That miracle must be Morrison's death.

At his rooms, he drugs and then exposes the unconscious Morrison to gas, killing him, without causing suspicion. He is given the championship medal by default. As winner he is invited to a major tournament in Budapest. At the match, he is playing brilliantly, in sight of victory in his first match, until he sees Morrison enter and invisibly guide his opponent's hand, after which he smiles at Pownall. The match goes on, dazzlingly, relentlessly, an event to be recorded and remembered in chess annals, but Pownall is doomed. Game after game the charade is repeated. He demonstrates his brilliance, and yet is always defeated, with the smiling Morrison standing behind and subtly leading his opponents.

He returns to London, but even in his private chess club, the smiling Morrison enters. Pownall knows suicide is the only answer. He leaves behind a complete record of the events, describing every chess move of those games. Then, writing the last words even as the still smiling Morrison enters his room, his final sentence is left incomplete.

The papers eventually reach a chess player, who discovers that no record of the professor's ever playing at the British match exists. Nor was there even a match at Budapest that year! However, studying the moves, he is astonished at their brilliance. He memorizes them. Later, in a competition, he begins using the sensational moves. A stranger enters and stands behind his opponent. When his opponent moves, he seems strained and puzzled. And in turn, when he reaches to move, the hand that makes the move is not his own. He suggests the game be called a draw, which is immediately accepted, and retires to his room, where he burns the papers with all their brilliant plays. Two shadows from the corner appear to grow vast and fill the room, but the papers suddenly blaze and they are gone. And with them, happily, his memory of their plays.

It is a little tale, but a tour de force which, while amusing the reader, offers as well that "odd, insinuating little sensation." The characterizations within its dozen pages are perfect to its purposes, and each word counts. Surely a chess devotee might well be envious of the opportunity the player was given, but might equally well agree with his ultimate decision.

If chess was the sport of "Professor Pownall's Oversight," golf is the subject, obviously, of "The Seventeenth Hole at Duncaster." Again, there is an ironic humor which underlies the developing horror of this tale of the links, perhaps because Wakefield was himself a true golfing enthusiast and enjoyed his private joke at his fellow-players' expense. The 17th hole is a newly created one, hacked through an ancient grove of trees, on a small mound that was once a place sacred to the Druids. Several people will die most awfully there, their deaths predicted mockingly in dreams to the club secretary.

Wakefield would continue to write ghost stories for nearly forty more years, and as might be expected, there would be stylistic changes in that time. They were not evident as yet, however, in his next book, published in England a year later as *Old Man's Beard / Fifteen Disturbing Tales*. The title was changed in the American edition to *Others Who Returned*, which, like the title of the first book, referred directly to the nature of the contents and provided a properly eerie ambience.

The narrative style is as crisp, the spines of the plots as straight and uncomplicated, and the chills as cold. In "Look Up There" Mr. Packard, who is vacationing to give his jangled nerves a rest, is annoyed by a little man who, at all times, even during dinner, seems to be staring upward at a 35-degree angle. His constant companion, a taciturn "yokel," ignores his friend's mannerism. One day, outdoors, the man tells Packard his chilling tale of a manor famed as much for its ballroom and picture gallery, as for being haunted only on New Year's Eve. On such a dire occasion, as an occultist, he had come to observe a party held by new tenants. It had become feverish, even hysterical, and the little man, sensing a growing pressure, had run off to his bedroom. At midnight came a mighty tolling of the clock. Suddenly it ceased, and then he heard a woman's piercing scream: "Look up there!". . .upon which every light in the house had gone out.

With a flashlight in hand, he had nervously gone down. There sat the entire company, rigid, mouths flecked with foam, and eyes wide open, focused on the door into the Long Gallery. "And then I flashed my torch up toward the door into the Long Gallery, and there—and there—"

A dazzling flash of lightning and a crash of thunder interrupt his story. He hurls his arms up, and begins screaming "Look up there! Look up there!" Mr. Packard moves to him, but the yokel is suddenly alert, grasping the little man. "Leave him to me," he shouts, "I know what to do" and pushes him back toward the hotel, their progress punctuated by shouts from the little man of "Look up there!" And what was it that the little man had seen, that fateful New Year's Eve, through the door into the Long Gallery? Wakefield does not say.

The reader may be reminded of Michael Arlen's classic horror story "The Gentleman from America," in which a man's madness is only perceived at the end. The significant difference is that whereas the American has accepted as his own a story which did not actually involve him, the little man's tale of the horror beyond the Gallery door may have been true. The beauty inherent in a tale which achieves its aim by suggestion is its tantalizing incompleteness, ever beguiling and bedeviling. This would not work in a tale of many twistings, but in the direct stories the author was writing at this time, it is always feasible.

Very direct, in this volume, is "Blind Man's Buff," a terrifying nightmare in which Wakefield uses tellingly that most basic of fears—fear of the dark. A man who is considering purchase of a vacant, centuries-old manor reaches it rather late in the day; still, he must have a look. Within, he feels in the dark for the light-switch; he cannot find it. Nor can he find matches in his pocket. Deciding he must have left them in his car, he goes back to the door.

In the darkness, he cannot find the door. He feels for it along the wall, but simply cannot find it. His efforts remain unavailing, and to give himself pause from this impossible mystery, he tries to sit and rest for a moment. *Something,* however, seems to brush against him. His fears mount. He just cannot find the door! The author thus tops our fears of the dark by a *coup de grace*—the sense of claustrophobia: "And then he ran screaming round the room; and suddenly his screams slashed back at him, for he was in a little narrow passage."

Despite his busy profession at this time, in the later 1920s, as a publisher, Wakefield became an increasingly prolific writer, with non-fantastic books as well. Two such, *Gallimaufry* and *Happy Ever After,* appeared in 1928 and 1929 respectively. His next collection of short stories, *Imagine a Man in a Box,* was published in 1931. The somewhat playful title would indicate a broadening approach, with less dependence on the classic ghostly tale format. They amble a bit more than the earlier stories, although some tend to return to earlier gambits of supernatural fiction, such as the dead seeking vengeance. Such shades, perceived only very dimly in previous stories, are rather more distinct here, particularly in an ironic story such as "Damp Sheets."

Dear, wealthy, and ow dead Uncle Samuel actually makes such a reappearance, briefly, and adequately. His wastrel nephew's wife had managed to hasten Uncle Samuel's demise by placing damp sheets and a leaking water bottle in his bed while he was visiting in their home. One day when she goes to her linen closet, he returns the favor. She is discovered there later, suffocated by the sheets, which are unaccountably quite damp.

Despite the sardonic charm of the telling, it is fairly routine vengeance-of-the-dead stuff, lacking the delicately drawn horror, and none of the engenderend fear, of the earlier works. Such stories would be imitated to distraction by his admirer and American publisher, August Derleth, and a host of others, although John Collier would have delightfully rich and malicious fun with the get-rid-of-the-rich-uncle theme in "Another American Tragedy."

Wakefield had been a captain of infantry in the Royal Scots Fusiliers, 1914-1918, and had served both in France and in Macedonia. He reached the rank of captain. Memories of the Great War are recollected in another traditional type of supernatural tale—the clairvoyant or extrasensory. "Day-Dream in Macedon" is a slight tale, and perhaps a transmuted memory as well for the author. War fantasies were not uncommon. Arthur Machen's "The Bowmen" resonated in war-time Britain, and in America, A. Merritt's "Three Lines of Old French," while by no means more than a mere story in a popular magazine, reflected the same feelings—the need for hope in a trying period.

Lieutenant Eastleigh is stationed on the western front in France. He is very close to his superior, Captain Tennie, but because of his knowledge of Balkan languages is transferred to Salonika. Tennie writes now and then, always annoyed he has not gotten into action. Several years later Eastleigh is relaxing on leave at the River Struma in Macedonia. He has a sudden vision of "the Lys, near Croix-du-bac" and a terrible battle. Soldiers are attempting to cross a stone bridge. He recognizes one—Tennie. "He tried to shout to him, but he was in a region closed to sound. Yet Tennie saw him, waved to him, and smiled. Then something lashed down on him—he flamed like a torch" and Eastleigh finds himself staring at a golden oriole in a tree, and his eyes filled with tears.

After the war he dines in London with an old company mate, Spears, who describes last Tennie's battle. Nearly the entire company had been killed, but Tennie, leading, had just disappeared. "He took a direct hit just short of the bridge," Eastleigh murmurs "dreamily" and Spears puts down his knife and fork and stares at him.

The Green Bicycle Case, a book on criminology, appeared in 1932. That same year *Ghost Stories* was published, containing several new stories, but consisting primarily of stories already published. One, "Used Car," a spoof of the ghost story, even uses a Roaring Twenties Chicago gangster milieu. It is quite a distance from the traditional oak-paneled British manor house, for in this instance the *car* is the haunted house! The new owner of the car is fortunate to escape alive with his family, particularly when he learns that Blonde Beulah Kratz, a "well-known moll" (in Chicago) and her boyfriend, "a thirty-minute egg who tried to doublecross the rest of the gang" had been "taken for a trip" in it. Their intangible presence has remained. The story, several light years from "He Cometh and He Passeth By" nevertheless is amusing and by any odds the most unusual "haunted house" in the literature.

A mystery novel, *Hearken to the Evidence*, was published in 1934, followed the next year by *A Ghostly Company*. Again almost all stories that had appeared before. Several were new; like the few new stories in *Ghost Stories*, they were hardly unique or up to Wakefield's earlier level. "Death of a Poacher" is one. It is a grouping of every imaginable cliché about "the dark continent," with a protagonist who makes the unfortunate error of angering a witch-doctor. Later, back in England, he will pay the full and grim price.

Four years elapsed before the publication of another book of Wakefield supernatural stories, most of those collected this time new to hardcovers. *The Clock Strikes Twelve* was published in England in 1940 and its American edition, the first Wakefield collection to appear here in fifteen years, came off press in 1946. It was to be the first of two Arkham House collections of Wakefield stories. Furthermore, when August Derleth published it in 1946, four stories not appearing in the earlier British edition were added. (They had appeared in the several British collections prior to that.) It contained an introduction, "Why I Write Ghost Stories," as urbane and polished as the best of his fiction. Here he explains his experience with psychic phenomena and his personal belief in them. Derleth's admiration for Wakefield is evident, inasmuch as this was one of the earliest Arkham House imprints to feature short fiction by an author not of the *Weird Tales* magazine group.[7] In his personal life, Wakefield had by the late thirties become a full-time writer. In 1936 Wakefield was divorced by his first wife, Barbara Standish Waldo, an American woman he had married in 1920. In 1946 he married Jessica Sidney Davey, but had no children from either marriage.

Wakefield offers an amusing aside on the writing profession in "Not Quite Cricket," a story that appears in this volume. The major character is a writer, and in describing his writing technique, Wakefield, no doubt with tongue firmly in cheek, possibly describes himself: "When (Mr. Winter) got a story just right, everyone concerned knew there was very little for him to do about it. In fact, there were just three letters to write about it: one to his agent enclosing the story, another to his agent accepting the offered terms, and one to his bank enclosing the cheque. For Mr. Winter had a system. Sometimes he would write a story that completely satisfied him, sometimes one that he felt a shade uncertain about. He put those of the second sort straightway into the waste-paper basket. A simple system, but editors had so much reason to appreciate and trust it that they would write out a cheque even before reading the tale. And it is persons whom editors treat like that— about .9% of those writing tales—who make a good living out of the game. And Mr. Winter made £2000 a year at the game, which shows the great value of a system, if editors take any notice of it."

During World War II Wakefield served in London with the Home Forces; for the BBC he wrote plays and gave occasional talks. He had the misfortune of losing his home dring a Nazi air-raid near the end of the war. He did not stop writing, but, unlike the successful Mr. Winter, he had no further novels or collections, aside from the two Arkham House books.

The Clock Strikes Twelve is a conscious, and often successful, effort to return to the style of his earlier ghost stories. Its opening tale, "Into Outer Darkness," has, again, a haunted manor. It has its legend as well, of a man who had been walled up alive during the English Civil Wars. The new owner invites a clairvoyant friend to test it. The tale is brief, its horror being thereby attentuated, but the few paragraphs describing a candle-lit table of vaguely sensed judges, is effective, as is the all too sensitive friend's subsequent panic and suffocation. It is lean yet satisfactory Wakefield.

"The Alley" is a haunted house tale, economically, brilliantly told. The ancient house has a tragic past: in a small loft room called "the Alley" a farmer had, ages ago, tortured and driven mad his wife and daughter. In turn he was seized by the villagers and burned on a stake erected in the yard. A new owner and his friends find what must be the fateful "Alley," well-bolted, off a staircase. It is merely a passageway, six by twelve feet, with a single sealed window and a bench. Below the window they can see a small grassless patch. With unabated skill, Wakefield develops and fear and foreboding. There will be no spectral forms; the horror that comes upon two of them is the force of a terrible, undying past.

Sport, a favorite preoccupation of the writer, enlivens "Not Quite Cricket," a double entendre in the context of the story, and yet another tale of vengeance from the dead. It is weighty in the game's terminology, mystifying to a non-devotee, but an integral background to a supernatural tale told by an old codger sponging drinks from an amused writer of ghost stories. If the story is hardly classic, the laugh is at the end, when the writer admits to the bartender that the old man had told him a story he himself had written twenty years before. It is a raconteur's tale, and the ghostly interlude is an undistinguished part of the mechanism.

An interesting comparison with his earlier style is "Lucky's Grove," a pagan mysteries tale, as was "The Seventeenth Hole at Duncaster." Here a tree is taken from a "sacred" grove for a Christmas Day party in the newly acquired mansion of a *nouveau riche*. Unfortunate and unaccountable accidents occur, in an atmosphere of growing horror, soon to become terrifying and fatal. In its own right, the story is quite effective. Yet it was the direct, understated telling of "The Seventeenth Hole at Duncaster" that made it so memorable. It is burdened here with trite snobbery[8] and familiarity of theme. The ending itself is a final revenge by Loki (mentioned in a sub-title legend, and the real namesake of the grove) and the author alike on people neither of them likes.

It is noteworthy that in the various stories that Wakefield has written in which ghosts of ancient gods were disturbed, the victim had not wilfully sought to disturb or damage sacred places. It is chance, ignorance, or accident that brings doom. Wakefield, as quoted above, believes that ghosts are malignant, or, at least, that their effects upon human intruders will be, and therefore are best left alone.

In no other story is this better illustrated than in "Jay Walkers," a wry tale from this volume. In this instance, the ghosts of a young woman and her lover are walking on a country road. She expects to be his wife; he will be her murderer. The anniversary of the deed brings the pair back and, regrettably, motorists passing by at a particular hour, seeing the young people in their path, veer sharply, invariably into fateful accidents.

With the drably titled "Ingredient X," Wakefield leaves the classic vein of understated, vague spectral beings and moves into outright horror, explicit and shocking, and one of his most spine-chilling stories. In a triumph of *guignol*, the author drenches the story in blood: a blood-soaked body of a dog; a terrifying eyeless figure with blood gushing from its throat; and a hero who wakes in his bed thinking with gratitude that he must have been having a nightmare until, in the darkness, as he reaches for matches next to his bed, his hand touches something "swilling up over his wrist." He smells a terrible stench, which he has previously smelled without having been able to identify it, but now he knows it for blood. Next morning he leaves. Some time later, the young man, more satisfactorily quartered, will think back, and the author will have one final triumph of fright.

Arkham House had promised a new collection of Wakefield's work "for early publication" on the dust jacket biography of the writer. In fact, it was not until 1961 that his final collection, *Strayers from Sheol,*[9] appeared. In England his work had become neglected. Such stories of his that were published were appearing in the late 1940s in the short-lived Arkham House magazine *The Arkham Sampler,* as well as *Weird Tales, Magazine of Fantasy and Science Fiction,* and *Fantastic Universe.* For his final book, these stories were collected, and several others not previously printed in America were added. Most of the stories had been written prior to 1953. By 1961, Wakefield was ill. Although he still did occasional writing, he would die four years later of cancer. His introduction to the collection, "Farewell to All Those!" commences: "I've written my last ghost story." And having written more than one hundred of them, he feels he knows what he is talking about when he adds "I believe ghost story writing to be a dying art. It's possible another Montague Rhodes James may appear some day, but I profoundly doubt it. . .he closed an epoch." Concerning psychic matters, he says "Science has usurped their function, and, I suppose, made a mockery of it."

This final volume is uneven. It cannot pretend to have the fresh yet classic qualities of his first book, with its subtle horror, but several of the stories are splendid in their own manner. The older writer here is perhaps, as he has stated, more skeptical, too far removed from the ghosts he once had known. The more direct ghost stories fall back on mechanics of the genre. In particular, there is a preponderance of revenge-of-the-dead stories. While they represent an ingenious group of variations on that theme, they also move in the path of Wakefield's late-found graphic physical violence. The appetite of the dead for retribution has become voracious. Several tales, however, represent a new departure, stories only tenuously supernatural, possibly psychological, in the manner of Henry James' "The Turn of the Screw."

85

"The Third Shadow" is such a vengeance story in a rather unusual setting—mountain climbing. The climber who deliberately caused the death of his inexperienced wife in an apparent climbing accident, is eventually himself killed while climbing with a friend. Some onlookers say a third shadow was seen along the rope with the two men. "The Middle Drawer" features a parsimonious man who has been exonerated in the sudden death of wife. Her ghost disturbs him as well as his new romance, and a drawer in a bureau has a queer habit of "shooting open" quite by itself. Within it is the cyanide he has not brought himself to throw away. Another is "Woe Water," this time with a pair of successive ghosts, each of whom would seem to have been the victim of the diarist telling the story. Although he protests his innocence throughout, he is hanged for the murder of the second. Did their restless spirits bring him the doom he deserved, or was his diary honest, and Fate the cheat? Yet again, the unseen ghost in "Four-Eyes" gains vengeance against his poisoning wife via a pair of apparently ordinary spectacles. Her new husband finds them in a desk and they are a fine fit. When, however, he has worn them long enough, he begins to relive her late husband's last hours. She understands at once, grabs the glasses away, and goes out to dispose of them. He hears her scream and runs out. She is dead, her eyeless face bloody and splintered with glass shards.

Leaving the seemingly ubiquitous vengeful ghosts for a more characteristically ghostly tale, "Ghost Hunt" has the gimmick of being a live radio broadcast. It thus has immediacy and eventually a very personal shock value. It could well be performed as a radio drama, and although it first appeared in print in *Weird Tales* March 1948, perhaps Wakefield had intended it for one of his B.B.C. plays. A notorious haunted house is visited by a radio program, graphically described by the announcer and a professor recognized for his investigations of psychic phenomena. Although the devotee of the genre knows each will come to a bad end, the story is well told. The announcer will discover blood as well as the body of the professor, reciting his progress in a mad singsong to his radio listeners.

One may compare the story to the classic Charlotte Perkins Gilman (Stetson) short story "The Yellow Wall Paper." Here the heroine and narrator goes mad within her room, and, in the final moment of shattering horror, creeping around it in endless circles, bemoans her husband's having fainted right within her path.

86

Wakefield's announcer discovers the professor's body when he too is already mad, and is as blithe about it. Were there ghosts, and were there any in the swirling patterns of the wallpaper? We are not told.

"A Kink in Space-Time" is an unusual ghost story inasmuch as the unfortunate protagonist meets the ghost of himself after his death-to-come. Edgar Allan Poe and H.P. Lovecraft in their short stories "William Wilson" and "The Outsider," and James Gould Cozzens in his remarkable novel, *Castaway*, offer variations of the theme, accomplished with more verve. Wakefield's man is a disturbed individual, and it is possible that it was all a fiction of his mind.

"The Gorge of the Churels," certainly one of the book's—and Wakefield's—finest stories, had appeared on August Derleth's recommendation a decade earlier in *The Magazine of Fantasy and Science Fiction*, October 1951. There Anthony Bucher wrote of Wakefield that he "stood in somewhat the same relation to the old master M.R. James as James to the still Older Master Sheridan Le Fanu" and the story is "as subtle and complex as anything he's done." It is an ironic and sensitive account of an outing of a British family and their manservant, an Indian, bringing to memory the cavern sequence of E. M. Forster's *A Passage to India*. Here at a gorge, the ghosts, or "Churels," of women who die in childbirth "continue to haunt the earth, with a view to seizing the soul of some living child and carrying it off to the void to comfort them." The British couple laugh at the notion and walk off, bearing with them the insufferable arrogance of the conqueror. Behind them the little Indian watches their child play and rankles with inferiority. "He would like to see these people punished for their vanity and stupidity." And the worst punishment would be the loss of their child. Then he senses the presence of someone, something.

The moment calls forth the author's finest sensitivities and the result is haunting. "Just to the left of the basin was a circular grove of mulberry trees, and at the centre of this circle was something that had no business to be there, at least so it seemed to Mr. Sen. The sun's rays coiling between the leaves dappled and, as it were, camouflaged this intruder, so that it appeared just a thing of light and shade; like every other visible entity in the world, of course, yet somehow this was essentially incorporeal, not linked to earth, but painted thinly on the freckled air.

Sen watches, as child and apparition near one another, and he is "aware of a horrid tension in the air, like the swelling potential before the lightning stroke." But, as the child sees something there and innocently runs towards it, Sen cannot allow it, and leaps up shouting incantations. "Little Nikky paused, glanced round and fell on his face, and the thing of light and shade seemed to lose its form and pass into the stippled air." Hearing the noise the parents run in and are reassured. Sen says he shouted at a bad dream. Mr. Prinkle mocks him, asking whether he dreamed of "those bereft and acquisitive Churels." Sen in turn laughs. "It is not fair of you, Mr. Prinkle, to pull my legs so, and remind me of the ridiculous superstitions of us poor ignorant, primitive Indians!"

In yet another variation on the ghost story, Wakefield utilizes the form as a means of characterization; such is the case with "Monstrous Regiment." It is a harrowing if uneven tale of a man with a dying wife, who brings in an eighteen-year-old girl as governess for his seven-year-old son. She quickly becomes mistress to the man but her real interest, and it is pointedly erotic, is the boy, a "quite perfect little man" to her. The mother soon dies, hating the girl, who now establishes her dominance in the household. She carefully rears the boy so that he will one day gratify her insatiable sexual appetite. When he is thirteen, she sees to it. Her demands weaken him and he hates her even while he knows she is all he can ever want. Well into the tale, his mother appears to him, urging him to kill the girl. He does it by causing an elecrical apparatus to fall into her bath. He is overwhelmed, however, by a sense of loss, and collapses. When he awakes he is institutionalized, too young to be charged with murder. Here he writes this memoir, abuses his attendants, and then abruptly dies, still a young man, of a cerebral hemorrhage.

The appearance in the story of his mother's ghost comes almost gratuitously. Was it real to him, or was it the product of his needs, to blame her for his love/hatred of the girl, who filled and abused his life until nothing more could be made of it? Bleiler[9] compares this type of story to Robert Aickman's "strange stories," fantasies frequently filled with symbolism and enigmatic, unanswerable questions. One may compare "Monstrous Regiment" to "The Swords," in which a young and sexually inexperienced young man attends a carnival sideshow and watches men plunging swords into a bored young woman, one after the other, somehow causing no harm. When his turn comes, he slips out. The girl comes to his rooms, however He fumbles for sexual union, while she is more or less supine, and suddenly her arm comes off in his hand. She gets up now, sobbing, dresses, grabs at him, for the arm apparently, and leaves.

The story offers no answers, only puzzles. It exists in its inexplicable state, its metaphors reaching into the reader's deeper mind for explanations. Wakefield does not attempt this with such explicit fantasy as Aickman, although he seems to be on the verge of such strange and outrageous symbols as Aickman's. It is also beyond the Henry James psychological query as to whether it is fantasy or truth, because it does not matter here. Only the characters matter, not the supernatural element. The story is unpleasant, but there is strength in its direct, graphic narration. It is a far cry from his simpler ghost stories. This tendency is continued in "Immortal Bird," which, an apparent revenge of the dead story, tells of an ambitious man who has a buried and possibly justified sense of guilt. He may have caused the death of an aging professor who had refused to resign his chair to him. The many birds that inhabit the old man's garden had loved him and are an obvious and implacable symbol of his successor's guilt; in trying to destroy them he must destroy himself.

The texture of this later work is more dark and complex than those early and direct tales. Always a splendid technician of words, Wakefield remained as capable of producing an uncomfortable sensation of chilliness along the spine decades after he began this daunting task. Unfortunately, although Arkham House promised a third Wakefield collection, it was not forthcoming. There would not be many tales after *Strayers from Sheol*. During his final years those few were published by August Derleth in anthologies of new fiction. In 1962, "The Animals in the Case" appeared in *Dark Mind, Dark Heart*, and in 1964 "The Last Meeting of Two Old Friends" in *Over the Edge*, each among his finest in his later style. In the former, a domineering one-eyed goose is a symbol to a man of his late and beloved mother, who had killed both her lover and herself. The latter, delightfully ironic in tone, yet superbly atmospheric, finds new breath in that old chestnut of a locale, a cemetery. There are only hints of a ghost, never defined, and there are warnings to the hero by a gravedigger Hamlet would have appreciated. The climax arrives swiftly and horrifyingly and would appear to be less involved with the supernatural than with a bitterly jealous rival for his wife's love. Yet it is both.

Derleth would print two additional Wakefield tales posthumously, the second one, "Appointment With Fire," in *Dark Things*, 1971, a trivial but comic and satiric affair in the gangster style of "Used Car." The other, actually Wakefield's last story, found among his effects after he had destroyed most of this papers, was "Death of a Bumblebee," which appeared in *Travellers By Night* in 1967. It is a fitting climax to a career marked by consistently fine and durable writing, by a writer Derleth invariably referred to as "the dean of ghost story writers." The writing is at his most sophisticated level, erotically charged, more like his novels and plays than his ghost stories, but the driving element is among his most strange. The female protagonist is convinced, against all logic, that an unexploded World War II bomb lies directly beneath her home and will explode soon. Neither her husband nor their self-effacing friend who also loves her, nor her medical advisor, also attracted to her, can dissuade her. The bomb is the symbol of her digression into adultery, even of sexuality itself, her fear and her guilt. At the end, there is a shattering explosion and all perish. A bumblebee which has fluttered through the pages of the story is hurled from "the savoury depth of a *Gloire de Dijon* rose where it had been drowsily feasting." It manages to fly up but a bird catches it. "Too harsh for its taste, the little bird spat out the dying bumblebee." Consciously or otherwise, there is something of an epitaph here, for a writer who spent his last years for the most part ignored. H. Russell Wakefield died August 2, 1965.

In his preface to *Strayers from Sheol*, having been despondent about the possibilities of another M. R. James appearing one day, Wakefield decides his momentary defeatism should not, after all, prevent some new writer from snatching the "sinister torch" from his hand. His memories become warm, as he recalls a beloved M. R. James classic: "But look! Look! Those bedclothes forming into a horrid crouching shape!" and his own first and probably still dearest story: "Remember too those who galloped like crazed beasts from the Red House to their doom in the reeds! No, don't be too sure that none of the old magic endures!"

Notes

1. Quoted on the dust jacket of *Strayers from Sheol*, from the London *Daily Telegraph*, no date given.

2. Introduction, *The Clock Strikes Twelve*, Arkham House edition, pg. vii.
3. From H.P. Lovecraft's *Supernatural Horror in Literature*, reprinted in *Dagon and Other Macabre Tales*, Arkham House Publishers Inc., Corrected Fifth Printing, 1986, pgs. 416-17.
4. Introduction, *The Clock Strikes Twelve*, pg. xi.
5. *The Clock Strikes Twelve* was the twentieth book published by Arkham House. August Derleth's immediate intention with the house was to publish Lovecraft's works, and from this he began to publish one-author collections of stories that had been published in and characterized the magazine *Weird Tales*. Prior to the first Wakefield collection, the only non-*Weird Tales* writers to be published by Arkham House in such short story books were J. S. LeFanu's *Green Tea and Other Ghost Stories* (#12), Algernon Blackwood's *The Doll and One Other* (#15) and A. E. Coppard's Fearful Pleasures (#19). *Strayers from Sheol*, the second Wakefield book, would be Arham House's 60th book. A third collection, promised several times in Arkham House anthologies, did not materialize.
7. Wakefield, who attended Oxford University, has a special disdain for the *nouveau riche*, who have made money and are ostentatious about its use. It is a viewpoint frequently found in British literature, where these individuals are usually the butt of humor or barometers of social change. Wakefield employs them in his fortunate ability of being able to write supernatural humor. Less happy evidence of his class and racial attitudes is found on several other occasions. In "Used Car," Mr. Canning is waited upon by "a sprightly young Semite," which is a perhaps unnecessary qualification, but harmless. In the posthumously published "Appointment With Fire," however, the hapless gangster-protagonist Nathaniel Marks is cursed to his face as "a dirty kike" by an enemy. This is, of course, the character's prerogative. Unfortunately, the author later inserts without the benefit of conversation *his own* observation that "Mr. Bilker gazed down on the great gross Jew-boy." Perhaps the author allowed himself the liberties inasmuch as both stories are satiric and really quite comic. The far superior "The Last Meeting of Two Old Friends" has brief mention of its cemetery laborers as "niggers, Polacks, and Pats."
8. "Sheol" is the "Hebrew name for the abode of the dead or departed spirits," *Random House Dictionary of the English Language*, New York: Random House, 1967.
9. Everett F. Bleiler writes, concerning Wakefield's later stories, in *The Guide to Supernatural Fiction* (and is referred to in this respect by Jack Sullivan in his account of Wakefield in *The Penguin Encyclopedia of Horror and the Supernatural)* that they are "progressing from the simple Georgian story with a clear unitary theme to the modern more complex, partially symbolic story now best written by Robert Aickman." (Pg. 510)

References

The Guide to Supernatural Fiction, Bleiler, Everett F., Kent, Ohio: The Kent State University Press, 1983.

The Penguin Encyclopedia of Horror and the Supernatural, Sullivan, Jack, editor, New York: Viking, 1986.

The above books are indispensable as well as fascinating for the student of the genre. Bleiler offers specific notes about nearly every story by the numerous authors who constitute this genre, as well as a few key observations on the authors themselves. Sullivan offers a wide overview of the field, with brief essays on the lives and works of the authors, as well as films, plays, and other media forms pertinent to the field.

Contemporary Authors, Metzger, Linda, editor, Detroit: Gale Research Co., 1987. A multi-volume project and, in a world whose other author biography books do not find space for a great weirdiste, Ms. Metzer and staff offer nearly a full column, concise, compete and pertinent, and the source for the data presented here on the author's non-fantastic writings. It is further pointed out that "*Hearken to the Evidence* was made into a film of the same name; ten stories were adapted for radio and television in the United States, Europe, and Canada. His books have been translated into Dutch, French, Swedish."

The Best Ghost Stories of H. Russell Wakefield, selected and introduced by Richard Dalby, Chicago: Academy Chicago, 1982. This book is important for the student of Wakefield for several reasons: it is a superb selection, from each of his periods; it has a splendid introduction, the primary source for the biographical information presented in this paper; and, it is the only Wakefield book in print. Readers are urged to write the publishers at 425 N. Michigan Ave., Chicago, IL 60611, $5.95 plus postage, paperback.

I wuld also like to thank James Turner, the able successor to August Derleth as Editor of Arkham House publications, for permission to quote portions of Wakefield's writings from their two collections.

BOOKS BY H. RUSSELL WAKEFIELD

They Return at Evening: A Book of Ghost Stories, Philip Allan; London 1928

Gallimaufry, Philip Allan; London 1938 (non-fantasy).

Old Man's Beard: Fifteen Disturbing Ghost Tales, Geoffrey Bles; London 1929 (American title: *Others Who Returned: Fifteen Disturbing Tales,* Appleton, 1929).

Happy Ever After, Appleton, 1929 (non-fantasy).

Imagine a Man in a Box, Philip Allan; London 1931.
The Green Bicycle Case, Philip Allan; London 1932 (non-fantasy).
Ghost Stories, Jonathan Cape; London 1932.
Hearken to the Evidence, Doubleday 1934 (non-fantasy).
A Ghostly Company: A Book of Ghost Stories, Jonathan Cape; London 1934.
Landru, the French Bluebeard, Duckworth; London 1936 (non-fantasy).
Belt of Suspicion, Collins; London 1938 (non-fantgasy).
Hostess to Death, Collins; London, 1940 (non-fantasy).
The Clock Strikes Twelve: Tales of the Supernatural, Jenkins; London 1940.
American Edition, *The Clock Strikes Twelve,* Arkham House; Sauk City 1946.
Strayers from Sheol, Arkham House: Publishers; Sauk City 1961.
The Best Ghost Stories of H. Russell Wakefield, Selected and Introduced by
    Richard Dalby, J. Murray; London 1978. American edition, Academy
    Chicago; Chicago 1982.

THE LANDSCAPE OF SIN;
THE GHOST STORIES OF SHERIDAN LE FANU

Gary William Crawford

Joseph Sheridan Le Fanu (1814-1873) may be properly called the father of the English ghost story. Author of fourteen novels and nearly three dozen short stories, Le Fanu was the first writer to transform the conventions of Gothic fiction into a more intimate and personal form. His short stories of the supernatural, which were initially published as early as 1838, explore the Gothic mode and place it in urban settings. It is primarily Le Fanu's use of setting and atmosphere that provide a mental landscape in which sin, guilt, and supernatural retribution play prominent roles.

Le Fanu's life no doubt prepared him for the use of these themes in his fiction. The era in which he lived was increasingly troubled by questions about the existence of God and a supernatural order. Writing at the same time that Charles Darwin postulated his theories about evolution, Le Fanu was sensitive to a Victorian society struggling to maintain order and values in an era of industrialization and the consequent breakdown of traditional society. We know from his notebooks and correspondence that Le Fanu was a very religious man having difficulty coming to terms with a culture filled with radical doubt about revealed religion. His own wife Susan, who died in 1858 while still a young woman, repeatedly questioned the existence of God and faith in modern medicine.

Le Fanu was born in 1814 in Dublin, the son of a clergyman in the Church of Ireland, and his early life was spent in the country outside Dublin, where his father was rector of the church in Abington. Here Le Fanu witnessed factional fights among the peasants—between Protestant and Catholic Irishmen. Ireland's stormy existence served as an unsettling background for his fiction, and he saw his world decaying as the ascendant Protestant class was gradually losing its position in the country. Le Fanu had four children, was called to the Irish Bar, but did not practice law. Instead, he entered journalism, eventually becoming owner and editor of *The Dublin University Magazine*, in which most of his fiction was published.

The death of his wife was perhaps the most traumatic event of his life, as we know from a journal he kept during the time of her final illness. While it is unlikely that he became a recluse afterward, as legend would have it, he was forced to take upon himself the duty of raising his four children and supervising the most important newspapers in Ireland at the time.

Le Fanu's fiction may be divided into three periods. His first story was published in 1838 in *The Dublin University Magazine*. These tales of old Ireland are interspersed with a few ghost stories. In the 1840's he published two Irish historical novels, *The Cock and Anchor* and *The Fortunes of Colonel Torlogh O'Brien*. In Le Fanu's middle period, he published little, and not until 1861 did he turn to writing in earnest. Not only did he serialize his work in *The Dublin University Magazine,* but he also published fiction in such British magazines as Charles Dickens's *All the Year Round,* and in *Belgravia, London Society, The Dark Blue,* and *Temple Bar.*

Le Fanu made significant and innovative use of a mental and symbolic landscape in his ghost stories. He was well-read in the Gothic novel and was no doubt impressed by the fantastic imagery and the use of atmosphere in such works as Ann Radcliffe's *The Mysteries of Udolpho* and Charles Maturin's *Melmoth the Wanderer.* But, further, he also read the theological works of the eighteenth-century Swedish mystic Emanuel Swedenborg. Nearly all of Le Fanu's fiction can be read as Swedenborgian symbolic allegories in Gothic dress.

It is largely a "landscape of sin" that Le Fanu writes about in nearly all of his fiction, for he creates a landscape of the mind, in which symbols of the subconscious mind show a world in decay. Even in an early story such as "The Fortunes of Sir Robert Ardagh," a mental landscape of evil is depicted, as Sir Robert Ardagh is forced to his death by a mysterious valet who is, the story suggests, as evil as Satan himself. The story is rich and detailed, with strange omens, impressive atmosphere, and images of darkness and death. One might even say that valet Jacque is a figure out of one of Swedenborg's books.

Similarly, in "Schalken the Painter" Le Fanu shows his mastery in delineating atmosphere while building an impressive symbolic allegory around a painting by Godfried Schalken. The story has been regarded by some critics as the first genuine ghost story to transform the Gothic conventions into an urban and more intimate setting.

"The Watcher" ranks as one of the finest ghost stories of the mid-nineteenth century, as Le Fanu tells the story of Captain James

Barton who, in typical Le Fanu fashion, is an unbeliever, either in God or in supernatural agencies. But he is haunted to his death by the ghost of a man he had ordered punished by death years earlier. When Barton is engaged to be married, the ghost appears and, in a distinctly Swedenborgian touch, finally takes the shape of an owl. Here, Le Fanu has again transformed the Gothic props into a more intimate setting, creating a symbolic landscape in which animals, things, and people take on a terrifying and eerie meaning.

Even into the 1860's, Le Fanu's ghost stories continued to evoke Swedenborgian belief, in which the life of the spirit corresponded in a symbolic way to the natural. Not only does Le Fanu's body of work express such a relationship, but the predominant Swedenborgian themes of guilt and supernatural retribution appear as well.

Several stories, such as "An Authentic Narrative of a Haunted House," are presented as true accounts of the supernatural. Thus, Le Fanu's "new" ghostly fiction was a combination of several elements: the Gothic romance, Swedenborgian symbolism, nineteenth-century interest in spiritualism, and the sensation novel. The resultant synthesis raised the form of the ghostly in fiction to a whole new level.

The novella "The Haunted Baronet" is another reflection of the Gothic and of Swedenborg, for it is filled with supernatural incidents, strange dreams, and evil omens concerning the family history of Sir Bale Mardykes. Guilt, retribution, and death are the concerns that Le Fanu weaves throughout this complex narrative. It begins quietly enough as the setting of the village of Golden Friars is depicted in warm, friendly terms. Out of this "mental landscape," however, comes the tale's central supernatural incident: the appearance of a supernatural hand out of the haunted lake in the village. The hand symbolizes the past history of the Feltram and the Mardykes families and serves to signal evil. It brings about the death of Philip Feltram, but Feltram returns from the dead to haunt Sir Bale Mardykes so that he will return Mardykes Hall to the Feltram family.

The motif of the return of the dead "in power" is a repeated motif in Le Fanu's fiction. In "The Haunted Baronet" Philip Feltram returns from the dead vastly changed. In its symbolism and structure, it is reminiscent of one of Le Fanu's best novels, *Uncle Silas*, in which Swedenborgianism serves as the *modus operandi* of the entire book.

Swedenborgianism also figures directly in one of Le Fanu's most famous stories, "Green Tea," but with a difference. Over the years, his attitude toward the supernatural matured. Without a doubt, he retained his fascination with things spectral, but "Green Tea," one of the last ghost stories he wrote, is noteworthy for its ironic distance. Several critics have remarked on the irony of the tale, and it is one of the most strikingly modern ghost stories of the nineteenth century. One must read the story carefully to apprehend the delicate ambiguity. Arguably, the story is not a supernatural story at all. The monkey that haunts the Rev. Mr. Jennings may not be a supernatural creature at all, but may exist only in Mr. Jennings's mind. Here, Le Fanu brilliantly foreshadows the subtlety and distance of such twentieth-century masters of the ghost story as Ramsey Campbell. Nearly all of Campbell's ghost stories are about the nature of illusion, and surely Le Fanu was one of the first writers to explore this theme in spectral fiction.

In "Green Tea" the reader's perceptions are filtered through four different narrators, resulting in an extreme distance between the reader and the supernatural event. The story consists of one narrative within another, each further distorting the reader's view of what merely appears to be a supernatural occurrence; the structure creates Le Fanu's celebrated ironic distance.

Further, by basing the story on Swedenborg's occult-theological tenets, Le Fanu implies that Swedenborgian thought is only one more unreliable explanation of Jennings's experiences. Thus, Le Fanu creates a lingering doubt in the reader's mind about what actually happens to Mr. Jennings. It may be that the appearance of the monkey is merely a hallucination resulting from the narcotic effects of too much green tea; it may be, in the scientific-methaphysical jargon of Dr. Hesselius, who diagnoses Mr. Jennings, an opening of "the interior sense"; it may be one of the hellish creatures that Mr. Jennings reads about in the works of Swedenborg; and in psychological terms, it may be the symbolic representatin of Mr. Jennings's religious doubts. The point of all these conflicting possibilities is that none is unquestionably true. The supernatural occurrence is lost in a vortex of pain and horror, at the heart of which lies utter mystery.

In "Green Tea" we indeed find a mental landscape derived from Gothic fiction and the works of Swedenborg, but all is mystery; the nature of illusion, the difference between the subjective and objective are crucial.

Other stories by Le Fanu are more concrete explorations of sin and guilt, also derived from Swedenborg. For example, "Madam Crowl's Ghost" is narrated in the dialect of an Irish serving girl who comes to live at the home of an English family. The old beldame of the Crowl family dies in the girl's presence and returns from the dead to reveal a skeleton of a dead child, which is found behind a secret panel in the house.

Here, as in nearly all of Le Fanu's ghost stories, one finds the return of the dead from "the other life," the world of the spirit. In Swedenborg's philosophical system, one can penetrate the other life and find that it corresponds in a symbolic way to the natural world. Swedenborg also believed that the Bible was written in a symbolic and metaphorical language that corresponded to inner thoughts. Indeed, Swedenborg was one of the first great explorers of the subconscious mind, a precursor of Sigmund Freud and Carl Jung.

Writing at a time when the theories of the hypnotist Anton Mesmer had achieved great popularity, Le Fanu, like numerous other Victorian authors, was sensitive to the inner self. A story such as "Carmilla" may also be read as a story of the inner self, the "other life" of Swedenborg.

In "Carmilla" a castle in Styria and the ruins of the Karnstein castle nearby serve an obvious symbolic function in the landscape of sin. The castle of Laura and her father is the conscious or natural life, the ruins of Karnstein castle represent the darkness of the other life, the place of hell. From hell comes Carmilla, who is really Mircalla, Countess Karnstein, to vampirize Laura. We learn later that Carmilla is, like Laura, descended from the Karnsteins, and we may interpret her appearance and vampirization as a projection of Laura's mother, who died in her infancy. The symbolic and metaphorical play Le Fanu creates perfectly corresponds to the theories of Swedenborg and the properties of Gothic romance.

Early in the novella, Laura is expecting a friend to visit her, but she learns that the young girl has died. Immediately a coach accident occurs near the castle. A delicate young girl is hurt. The girl is Carmilla, whom Laura had seen in a dream when she was six. Carmilla stays with Laura and begins to vampirize her.

Carmilla may be taken as a symbol from the other life; her natural life name is Carmilla, but she is actually Mircalla, a vampire, a creature one reads about in Swedenborg's *Heaven and Hell*.

The inner life of the mind penetrates the other life of evil in an allegory of sin and death, mingling fear and desire. The world of sin, guilt, and retribution is brilliantly explored again and again in Le Fanu's fiction, in such ghost stories as "Mr. Justice Harbottle," in which a "hanging judge" dies after experiencing "the other life" where he is tried for the murder of the innocent while serving upon the bench.

While we are concerned here with only salient examples of the landscape of sin Le Fanu creates, his entire body of ghostly fiction may be read as allegory, employing the fantastic symbolism of the Gothic romance and the Swedenborgian philosophy for his own unique purposes. Le Fanu thus advanced the Gothic as no other nineteenth-century author, domesticating the mode and turning it to new and increasingly sophisticated purposes. His influence reaches to many later writers, most especially M. R. James (who tirelessly championed his cause), paving the way for the distinctly post-Gothic, twentieth-century manifestations of the ghostly tale.

Bibliography

Works by Le Fanu

Best Ghost Stories of J. S. Le Fanu. Ed. E. F. Bleiler. New York: Dover, 1964.
Ghost Stories and Mysteries. Ed. E. F. Bleiler. New York: Dover, 1975.
Uncle Silas. New York: Dover, 1966.
The Collected Works of Joseph Sheridan Le Fanu. Ed. Devendra P. Varma. New York: Arno Press, 1977.

Works about Le Fanu

Begnal, Michael H. *Joseph Sheridan Le Fanu.* Lewisburg, PA: Bucknell University Press, 1971.
Browne, Nelson. *Sheridan Le Fanu.* London: Arthur Barker, 1951.
McCormack, W. J. *Sheridan Le Fanu and Victorian Ireland.* Oxford: Clarendon Press, 1980.
Melada, Ivan. *Joseph Sheridan Le Fanu.* Boston: Twayne, 1987.
Sullivan, Jack. *Elegant Nightmares: The English Ghost Story from Le Fanu to Blackwood.* Athens, OH: Ohio University Press, 1978.

BLOOD BROTHERS
The Supernatural Fiction of A.C., R.H. and E.F. Benson

Mike Ashley

It is not unusual for several members of a family to be writers, the Waughs being a typical example, but it is perhaps a little unusual when three brothers should find solace and even a morbid fascination in occult and supernatural fiction. It's even more unusual when those three should be the sons of an archbishop of Canterbury. But such was the case with the Bensons: Arthur Christopher (1862-1925), Edward Frederic (1867-1940, known usually as Fred) and Robert Hugh (1871-1914, known always as Hugh). All three became prolific writers, and though none achieved his fame predominantly in the supernatural field, it is their horror fiction that has tended to survive beyond their more mundane efforts.

The most prolific of the three was Fred and he has also earned the most enduring reputation, chiefly through his humorous series of books about Lucia and Miss Mapp, two mischief-making females whose parishional exploits have recently gained renewed popularity in Britain. But the first to turn to writing and who in turn inspired the others, was Arthur.

Arthur was a natural scholar and academic and spent his whole life ensconced within the walls of academe (first Eton and later Cambridge). During the day he taught classics, but in the evenings he would be working on books, essays and countless letters, as well as a voluminous diary, perhaps the longest maintained by an individual. He had produced his first book soon after becoming a Master at Eton, a thinly disguised autobiographical novel called *Memoirs of Arthur Hamilton* (1886). Thereafter the bulk of his output was nonfiction, including studies of noted episcopalian and literary figures. There were also books of verse, starting with *Poems* (1893). Queen Victoria held him in high regard, treating him as an unofficial poet laureate in preference to the generally disliked Alfred Austin. Benson had achieved immortality, unrecognised by many, in the lyrics for "Land of Hope and Glory" which he wrote to accompany Edward Elgar's *Pomp and Circumstance March #1* when it was adapted for Edward VII's *Coronation Ode* in 1902. The song is now regarded as England's (as distinct from Great Britain's) national anthem.

The brothers' fascination with the supernatural may well have been imparted by their father, Edward White Benson (1828-1896). In his early days at Cambridge he had founded a Ghost Society which, through the work of his wife's brother, Henry Sidgwick, developed into the Society for Psychical Research. The elder Benson became something of an authority on hauntings and psychic phenomena. One case that came to his attention he reported to his close friend Henry James, who made use of it in his now classic story "The Turn of the Screw." There can be little doubt that Edward Benson would tell his children ghost stories, probably with a strong Christian moral, especially during the long winter evenings, and this was a tradition that Arthur continued. In the absence of his own children (none of the brothers married), Arthur's pupils at Eton were a more than adequate substitute. Every Sunday evening in winter, for about forty minutes before supper, Arthur would gather the boys of his House about him in his study and recount what became known as the Eton Nights' Entertainments. One of the pupils remembered these occasions with much fondness, adding that "No one who ever heard him could deny that he was a glorious story-teller."

Aware of the popularity of his stories, Arthur was finally persuaded to commit them to print. They appeared as two volumes, *The Hill of Trouble* (1903) and *The Isles of Sunset* (1904), both later reissued as the omnibus *Paul the Minstrel* (1911). They are mostly moral tales—"archaic little romances" Arthur himself called them—set in some unspecified medieval time and dealing with the deeds and dooms of various knights and priests. There is much of the mood of William Morris about them. Morris was, at the time of the tales' telling, working on his own fantasies—*The Wood Beyond the World* (1895) and others. While A.C. Benson had no great affection for Morris the socialist, he did admire Morris the writer and shared his love "for the kindly earth, and the simple country business."

Not all of the stories involve the supernatural—some are merely simple allegories—but all possess a glamor of the unworldly. There is no lack of vision or imagery in the stories, and Benson made full use of the many weird dreams that plagued him throughout his life and which he recorded in his diary. These dreams were always vivid and frequently unpleasant. One example, from February 1896, concerns a tramp whom he saw washing something over a well. He first thought it was a rabbit,

> but I presently saw that it was a small deformed hairy child,
> with a curious lower jaw, very shallow: over the face it had a
> kind of horny carapace... made of some material resembling
> pottery. I was disgusted at this but went on, and it grew dark: I
> heard behind me an odd sound and turning round saw this hor-
> rible creature, only a foot or two high, walking complacently af-
> ter me, with its limbs involved in ugly and shapeless clothes
> made, it seemed to me, of oakum, or some more distressing ma-
> terial. The horror of it exceeded all belief.

Both Arthur and Fred made good use of dreams as a device in
several of their stories, usually as portents. In Arthur's "The Gray
Cat," for instance, Roderick, the young son of a knight, while out
on his own one day, is strangely affected by a dark pool in the
hills. Thereafter he is plagued by dreams, first of two men emerging from the pool and claiming Roderick as their own, and then of
being trapped in the pool with the water rising. Roderick is only
released from his suffering after much tribulation. One is left to
wonder how much of A.C. Benson there is in the character of Roderick.

Perhaps the most memorable of Arthur's fireside tales is "The
Closed Window" which has much of M.R. James about it. James
was a close friend of the Bensons, particularly of Arthur, with
whom he had been a fellow scholar at King's College. "The Closed
Window" is set in the Tower of Nort, home of the good knight Sir
Mark and his cousin Roland. It tells of a room in the turret which
has been sealed shut since the bizarre death of Mark's grandfather,
who had lived at Nort under the blight of some strange shadow.
The tower room has four windows, one of which is locked and
barred and bears the inscription CLAUDIT ET NEMO APERIT [He
Shutteth and None Openeth]. One sunny day curiosity gets the
better of Mark, who opens the window to discover a world of
darkness with a bleak, rocky landscape and a shape "like a crouching man" that beckons him. At length it is Roland, not Mark, who
ventures into this world, resulting in one of Arthur's most effective
climactic scenes.

These moral tales mark the A.C. Benson of the 1890s and appear to be all that he intended to publish. That he continued to
create stories is certain, for he would occasionally join M.R. James

in his own legendary narration of Christmas stories. One such, "The House at Treheale," was related in 1903, and the manuscript was found along with others by Frederic, after Arthur's death. He published two of them under the title *Basil Netherby* (1927). These are more formalised ghost stories with one, "The Uttermost Farthing," being a splendid example of the haunted house genre. Both are studies in revenge and retribution as a result of dabbling in black magic, but these moral undertones are certainly secondary to the tale, unlike the earlier stories.

In selecting these two stories for publication Frederic had cast aside other, presumably less accomplished, items. Nevertheless, since these two examples show that Arthur was hitting his stride as a writer of ghost stories, one is left wondering what became of these other stories and whether more may survive. Arthur's association with M.R. James is enough to suggest that the two may have been mutually inspirational, and perhaps it is no surprise that Arthur's first two collections should appear at the same time as James's own *Ghost Stories of an Antiquary* (1904). Arthur had passed to Cambridge in 1903 as Master of Magdalen College and it seems more than likely that this closer association with M.R. James, who in 1905 became Provost of King's College, Cambridge, would have resulted in more stories. If so, where are they?

It is worth remembering that at this time Arthur was heavily involved in editing Queen Victoria's letters for publication, although this did not stop a stream of other essays flowing from his pen. In 1907, however, came the sudden mental collapse of his sister Maggie, and her removal to an asylum. This affected Arthur deeply, and he too slipped into a depression which lasted for two years. This melancholia did not lift until 1910 and then he returned to full college life and another active period of writing. He clearly retained an interest in the weird and wonderful, what with the reissue of his earlier stories as *Paul the Minstrel* in 1911 and the appearance of a sentimental religious fantasy about the immortality of the soul, *The Child of the Dawn* (1911). This work, which is uncharacteristically optimistic, had been prompted to a large degree by his brother Hugh's novels *The Lord of the World* (1907) and *The Dawn of All* (1911).

The period 1910/1911 was thus a creatively active one for A.C. Benson, and it has caused Jamesian scholar Rosemary Pardoe to wonder whether Benson might also be the identity behind the pseudonym 'B'. This graced seven short ghost stories published in the *Magdalen College Magazine* between 1911 and 1914. They do not read like Benson's other stories, but if written when emerging from a severe depression, may accountably be different. There are, however, certain stylistic similarities, but this and other circumstantial evidence is far from conclusive. Rosemary Pardoe published five of these stories in a booklet entitled *When the Door Is Shut* (1896) and interested parties may wish to investigate further. One of the stories, "The Strange Fate of Mr. Peach," is certainly worthy of A.C. Benson and it is hard to believe that, even if he were not 'B', he did not contribute in some way to the composition of these tales.

It is regrettable that A.C. Benson wrote no other works of horror or supernatural fiction. In 1917, after his sister's final decline and death, he entered a second and more intense bout of depression which lasted until 1922. He died of pleurisy on June 17, 1925, aged sixty-three.

Like Arthur, Hugh was plagued by moral and theological dilemmas. Hugh had been ordained a deacon in the Church of England by his father in 1894. The next few years saw him traveling to the Holy Land and Egypt as well as serving the poor in London before settling, in 1901, into a community life in the House of Resurrection at Mirfield, near Bradford, an Anglican establishment run on Benedictine lines. It was here, between evangelical work and study, that Hugh became fascinated with his brother Arthur's moralistic fantasies, and was inspired to compose the stories later published as *The Light Invisible* (1903). These are not stories in the formal sense, but rather episodes and incidents related by one priest to another, telling of odd, fleeting visions and matters unworldly. Few of the stories stand well on their own, possessing instead a collective atmosphere, although "The Traveller," in which the spirit of one of the knights who murdered Thomas à Becket still restlessly seeks absolution, has an individual merit.

Although the last of the Bensons to toy with the supernatural in fiction, Hugh was possibly the best of the three. His stories carry a sense of conviction that is absent from those by Arthur or Fred, and it is likely that Hugh had a greater experience of the occult than his brothers. He had, in his early days, been a Swedenborgian, and was keenly aware of the spirit world around us. In his later years he explored the psychic realms more actively, attending séances and performing exorcisms. For good measure he was also an accomplished hypnotist and there are grounds for believing that he experimented with drugs. In the days since his ordination Hugh had suffered much mental anguish about his calling, but while at Mirfield, he decided once and for all and in July 1903, instead of renewing his vows, he set himself on the path to Catholicism. Fired by a renewed enthusiasm and dedication, his progress was rapid and he received Holy Orders in Rome in 1904. This sudden conversion made Hugh something of a celebrity and his books became bestsellers, especially *By What Authority?* (1904), which questioned the very basis of the Church of England.

By 1907 Hugh had completed a second collection of stories in the same vein as the first but now reflecting a Catholic outlook. Though they are composed in a more traditional framework, the stories are heavy in propaganda which occasionally spoils moments of brilliance. Nevertheless this second volume, *The Mirror of Shalott*, has been singled out for praise by many for its singularity and inventiveness. Some of the stories are, again, mere episodes, but others, especially "Father Girdlestone's Tale" and "My Own Tale" have a power and intensity equal to any tales of the supernatural. Hugh may well have been drawing upon many of his own experiences, for there is a conviction about the stories that is chillingly effective.

Hugh's power as a writer is most evident in *The Necromancers* (1909), possibly his best work. It tells of a young man whose fiancée dies before their marriage. He joins a group of spiritualists in the hope of regaining her, only to find himself possessed by an evil spirit. The novel leaves no doubt as to Hugh's own views on the phenomenon: "Spiritualism is wrong," says Benson through one of his characters. "Evil spirits are at us all the time, trying to get in at any crack they can find. At séances...you open yourself as widely as possible to their entrance. Very often they can't get in, and then you're only bothered. But sometimes they can, and then you're done. It's particularly hard to get them out again." Elsewhere Hugh gives this sensible advice: "To go to séances with good intentions is like holding a smoking-concert in a powder-magazine on behalf of an orphan asylum."

Benson wrote a number of other novels, mostly thinly-veiled tracts of Catholic propaganda, of which the best known is probably *Come Rack! Come Rope!* (1912), with its convincing scenes of torture and religious persecution in Elizabethan England. Alas, Hugh's writing days were cut short by overwork, a weak heart and

. pneumonia. He died on October 19, 1914 aged only forty-two. Terrified of being buried alive, Hugh left strict instructions about his burial to ensure that he was unmistakeably dead before his interment.

Unlike Arthur and Hugh, E.F. Benson did not suffer from moral or theological issues. Although, like Arthur, he was plagued with vivid dreams, he was probably the most level-headed of the three. He was a wonderful athlete, with a fondness for winter sports, and had a wicked sense of humor with a delight in practical jokes. It would not be far from the truth to say that Fred never really grew up, and it was this that in all probability saved his sanity and allowed him to live a long and active life.

Fred was also inspired to write by his eldest brother's tale-tellings. He would occasionally sit in on the Eton Nights' Entertainments, and even used one of the stories as the basis for his later melodramatic novel *The Luck of the Vails* (1901), a murder mystery with only slight supernatural undertones. Fred's first attempt at fiction was, however, far removed from the supernatural. *Dodo* (1893) was, by Victorian standards, a rather risqué novel, portraying the rise of an ambitious if rather brainless "modern girl". The book delighted the scandalmongers of the decade and catapulted Frederic into the social limelight, a position in which he reveled. Thereafter he was determined to be nothing other than a writer, and spent the rest of his life trying to repeat his early success. It led to an output of over a hundred books, eighty of them works of fiction and only a dozen of those in the realm of fantasy.

Like Hugh, Frederic had his share of psychic experiences, and like Arthur, he had his share of dreams and nightmares. These, combined with his very active life, provided much fuel for his fiction, and it may possibly be why his horror stories, next to his humorous episodes of Mapp and Lucia, have survived when his many other books are forgotten.

Most of Fred's supernatural stories can be found in his major collections: *The Room in the Tower* (1912), *Visible and Invisible* (1923), *Spook Stories* (1928) and *More Spook Stories* (1934). The rest are tucked away in books and popular magazines of the day. Frederic did not set out to establish any special place for himself in the horror genre. If anything he is an imitator, lacking the conviction of Hugh and the intensity of Arthur, but with sufficient imagination and experience to lend his stories an individuality. He wrote ghost stories because he enjoyed that *frisson* of fear himself. He shared with Algernon Blackwood the belief that "the narrator must succeed in frightening himself before he can hope to frighten his readers." Perhaps for that reason he composed many of his stories in the first person.

When he came up with an idea that he liked, he was not averse to using it again and again. As a result a steady diet of E.F. Benson, unless selected carefully, can pall. In some stories Fred let the bare boards show through, with too little attempt to make them convincing (try for example, "And the Dead Spake—", an utterly absurd story in which a man likens the human brain to a gramophone record and tries to replay deep-seated memories). But these are minor infractions which one must expect from an author as prolific as Benson. They are far outweighed by his more polished and inventive tales. In all he wrote about seventy ghost and horror stories, some fifty of which are of high quality.

One fine example is "The Room in the Tower," the title story of his first collection. It grows out of a recurrent dream which plagues the narrator's adolescence and early manhood, but which never reaches a conclusion. The narrator only knows that he enters a room in a tower and is confronted by something terrible. At length the events in the dream begin to enact themselves in reality, and the narrator finds himself in the room. Awakened in the pitch darkness of night during a storm, he sees fleetingly in a flash of lightning "a figure that leaned over the end of the bed watching me," wearing a "close-clinging white garment, spotted and stained with mold." In the stygian blackness and deathly stillness that follow, he hears "the rustle of movement coming nearer."

Here Frederic is genuinely frightening himself and hoping to chill others. As in Arthur's stories, dreams are used to good effect. In "The Face" events are replayed almost scene for scene as a young girl's recurrent dreams lead inevitably to her doom, whilst in "Caterpillars" and "How Fear Departed from the Long Gallery" they serve as preludes to climactic events. Frederic was also much taken by the theme of fate, of one's unswervable destiny, both in life and beyond. It recurs most pointedly in "The Outcast," which makes full use of an idea almost tossed away at the end of "The Room in the Tower," that of a coffin that refuses to be buried. In "The Outcast" we follow the life and death of Mrs. Acres, whose body houses a spirit cursed in a former life never to rest or find shelter. As a consequence all things reject Mrs. Acres, and even after her death on board ship, when she is buried in the English Channel, the sea will not allow her rest, and she is cast up on the shore. When again laid to rest in the local churchyard, even the earth rejects her.

Unlike some of Benson's contemporaries, who left much unsaid, Frederic liked to dwell on grotesque and gruesome details, as in "The Horror Horn," where an Alpine form of Yeti has particularly nasty eating habits. Benson's greatest predilection was for things glutinous and slimy, especially worms and slugs. They appear as the manifestation of evil in several stories. "Negotium Perambulans," which H.P. Lovecraft thought possessed "singular power," is really a rather weak attempt at imitating M.R. James. It presents a remote Cornish village with a house cursed by an ancient evil in the form of a gigantic slug which sucks the body of all its blood. In "And No Bird Sings" we find a wood devoid of all animal and bird life due to the presence of an elemental. Two men set out to rid the wood of this unseen evil and find themselves assailed by something "cold and slimy and hairy," like a giant worm. The same sluglike elemental reappears in "The Thing in the Hall" while the victim in "The Sanctuary' is afflicted by a grey worm. Psychologists may well interpret the constant reference to worms as a reflection of Benson's own suppressed sexuality (interestingly, worms also turn up in Arthur's story "The Slype House") but they nevertheless serve as a profound store for horror tales. The frequent reworking of the device does tend to diminish any authentic terror, but there is one story in which Frederic employed the theme to stunning effect, "Caterpillars," which many regard as his best horror story.

Set, for once, in an Italian villa, it tells of the terrifying dreams that the narrator suffers. First, entering an unoccupied bedroom, he sees that the four-poster bed is a mass of writhing greyish-yellow caterpillars, all a foot or more in length and with crab-like pincers instead of suckers. The caterpillars become aware of his presence and turn their attention to him, pursuing him back to his own room. The next day just such a caterpillar is found by another of the guests, a painter called Inglis. The following night the narrator suffers another dream, and this time is forced to witness a relentless tide of caterpillars as they mount the stairs and force their way into the painter's bedroom. Later the symbolic significance of "the crab-like pincers" is brought to home when the narrator learns that from that second evening on, Inglis has contracted cancer.

This delight in overt horrors did not mean that Benson was immune to the more sensitive treatment of fear. Two of his best stories benefit from a controlled heightening of tension. "How Fear Departed from the Long Gallery" is, at the outset, a humorous story, with the occupants of a haunted house having accepted and actually delighting in the presence of a whole family of ghosts. However, Benson subtly converts the humor into fear with the inclusion of a curse related to the ghosts of twin children. These two ghosts are always avoided until, by misfortune, one of the occupants is forced to face them. "Pirates" is a beautiful evocation of childhood memories and how they return to haunt a man, who is endeavoring to recapture the past, in his final moments. The first was Benson's own favorite of his stories, whilst "Pirates" is arguably the most aesthetically successful.

Being so prolific, E.F. Benson turned to most of the traditional horror themes for his stories. "Mrs. Amsworth," for instance, is a fairly typical vampire story. "The Man Who Went Too Far" explores nature-mysticism, rather common in late Victorian fantasies, especially in the work of Arthur Machen and later Algernon Blackwood. Benson expanded this story into his novel *The Angel of Pain* (1905). "In the Tube" and "The Bed by the Window" show that he shared with H.G. Wells and again Algernon Blackwood a fascination for time and other dimensions. "Gavon's Eve" and "The Sanctuary" use witchcraft and other black magic as their central theme, while there are any number of stories involving séances and spiritualism. A later novel, *Across the Stream* (1919), joined with Hugh's earlier *The Necromancers* in its anti-Spiritualism message. Again it uses dreams as a vehicle for spirit manifestation, and carries an added sense of verisimilitude in Frederic's references to the protagonist's long-dead elder brother Martin. Frederic had himself had an elder brother Martin, who had died when Martin was only eleven.

Frederic's post-graduate days as an archeologist in Egypt and Greece provided the background for a few stories. "At Abdul Ali's Grave" involves an Egyptian black magician, whilst the novel *The Image in the Sand* (1905) combines Egyptian mysticism with spiritualism in a tale of a vengeful Egyptian spirit.

Frederic's novels, whilst not as accomplished as his short stories, are unjustly neglected. These include *Colin* and *Colin II* (1923/1925), really one long novel published in two parts, which studies the successive generations descending from a man who sold his soul to the devil in exchange for worldly power. *The Inheritor* (1930) is similar in that it involves a curse which manifests itself in alternate generations in the shape of cloven-hoofed, misshapen heirs. This novel contains some of Benson's best writing. Yet only *Raven's Brood* (1934), his last weird novel, has seen any recent revival, and even then it was misrepresented as a typical paperback gothic, complete with lighted turret window and backward-glancing fleeing maiden on the cover.

Although Benson's best-known short stories are those, like "Caterpillars," relying on more overt horrors, in due time his reputation must rest on his more subtle ghost stories. He rang the changes possibly more than any other author on the haunted house theme, and Benson's special variant, the haunted garden. Apart from "How Fear Departed from the Long Gallery" and "Pirates," the best examples of these two appoaches, Benson also wrote "Reconciliation," "The Gardener," "A Tale of an Empty House," "Expiation," and "Naboth's Vineyard"—amongst the best of a score or more of haunting tales.

In his final years, old, crotchety and crippled by arthritis, Fred spent less and less time writing. He was now a key part of the life of Rye, a lovely town in Sussex, where he lived in the former house of Henry James, and where he served as mayor from 1934 to 1937. He was also awarded the Order of the British Empire. He had installed in the parish church two beautiful stained glass windows, the first in 1928 in memory of Arthur, the second, in 1937, dedicated to his parents. The last, the west window, includes the figure of E.F. Benson himself in his mayoral robes. What other writer of ghost stories has such a shining memorial?

E.F. Benson died in London in February 29, 1940, whilst undergoing surgery. He was seventy-two, the last of the Benson brothers, each of whom had lived within his own private world. It is perhaps fitting that today we remember them for their dreams and fantasies.

BIBLIOGRAPHIES

A.C. BENSON

Short Fiction

The Hill of Trouble, London: Isbister, 1903. Contains "The Hill of Trouble," "The Grey Cat," "The Red Camp," "The Light of the Body," "The Snake, the Leper and the Grey Frost," "Brother Robert," "The Closed Window," "The Brothers," "The Temple of Death," "The Tomb of Heiri," "Cerda," "Linus."

The Isles of Sunset, London: Isbister, 1904. Contains "The Isles of Sunset," "The Waving of the Sword," "Renatus," "The Slype House," "Out of the Sea," "Paul the Minstrel," and "The Troth of the Sword."

Paul the Minstrel, London: Smith, Elder, 1911. Omnibus of the above two volumes.

Basil Netherby, London: Hutchinson, 1926. Contains "Basil Netherby" and "The Uttermost Farthing."

Note also: *When the Door Is Shut* by 'B', Runcorn, Cheshire: Haunted Library, 1986. Contains "The Strange Case of Mr. Naylor," "When the Door Is Shut," "The Strange Fate of Mr. Peach," "Quia Nominor," and "The Hole in the Wall."

Novel

The Child of the Dawn, London: Smith, Elder, 1911.

R.H. BENSON

Short Fiction

The Light Invisible, London: Isbister, 1903. Contains "The Green Robe," "The Watcher," "The Blood-Eagle," "Over the Gateway," "Poena Damni," "Consolatrix Afflictorum," "The Bridge over the Stream," "In the Convent Chapel," "Under Which King?" "With Dyed Garments," "Unto Babes," "The Traveller," "The Sorrows of the World," "In the Morning," "The Unexpected Guest."

A Mirror of Shalott, London: Sir Isaac Pitman, 1907. Contains "Monsignor Maxwell's Tale," "Father Jenk's Tale," " Father Meuron's Tale," "Father Brent's Tale," "Father Bianchi's Tale," "Father Stein's Tale," "Mr. Bosanquet's Tale," "The Father Rector's Tale," "Father Girdlestone's Tale," "Father Martin's Tale," "Father Macclesfield's Tale," "Mr. Percival's Tale," "Father Maddox's Tale" and "My Own Tale."

Novels

Lord of the World, London: Sir Isaac Pitman, 1907.
The Dawn of All, London: Hutchinson, 1911.
The Necromancers, London: Hutchinson, 1909.

E.F. BENSON

Short Fiction

The Room in the Tower, London: Mills & Boon, 1912. Contains "The Room in the Tower," "Gavon's Eve," "The Dust-Cloud," "The Confession of Charles Linkworth," "At Abdul Ali's Grave," "The Shootings of Achnaleish," "How Fear Departed from the Long Gallery," "Caterpillars," "The Cat," "The Bus-Conductor," "The Man Who Went Too Far," "Between the Lights," "The Terror by Night," "Outside the Door," "The Other Bed," "The Thing in the Hall," "The House with the Brick-Kiln."

The Countess of Lowndes Square, London: Cassell, 1920. Contains 14 stories, of which "The Case of Frank Hampden," "Mrs. Andrew's Control," "The Ape" and "'Through'" are supernatural.

Visible and Invisible, London: Hutchinson, 1923. Contains "'And the Dead Spake—'", "The Outcast," "The Horror-Horn," "Machaon," "Negotium Perambulans," "At the Farmhouse," "Inscrutable Decrees," "The Gardener," "Mr. Tilly's Séance," "Mrs. Amworth," "In the Tube," "Roderick's Story."

Spook Stories, London: Hutchinson, 1928. Contains "Reconciliation," "The Face," "Spinach," "Bagnell Terrace," "A Tale of an Empty House," "Naboth's Vineyard," "Expiation," "Home, Sweet Home," "'And No Bird Sings'", "The Corner House," "Cortophine," "The Temple."

More Spook Stories, London: Hutchinson, 1934. Contains "The Step," "The Bed by the Window," "James Lamp," "The Dance," "The Hanging of Alfred Wadham," "Pirates," "The Wishing Well," "The Bath Chair," "Monkeys," "Christopher Comes Back," "The Sanctuary," "Thursday Evenings," "The Psychical Mallards."

Two retrospective collections are:

The Horror Horn, St. Alban's: Panther books, 1974. Selected with an Introduction by Alexis Lykiard. Contains "The Room in the Tower," "Gavon's Eve," "Caterpillars," "The Thing in the Hall," "The House with the Brick-Kiln," ""The Horror-Horn," "Negotium Perambulans," "Mrs. Amworth," "The Face," "'And No Bird Sings'", "The Bed by the Window," "Monkeys," "The Sanctuary."

The Tale of an Empty House, London: Black Swan Books, 1986. Selected by Cynthia Reavell with an Introduction by Susan Hill. Contains "The Face," "Caterpillars," "Expiation," "The Tale of an Empty House," "The Bus-Conductor," "How Fear Departed from the Long Gallery," The Other Bed," "The Room in the Tower," "Mrs. Amworth," "'And No Birds Sing'", "Mr. Tilly's Séance," "Home, Sweet Home," "The Sanctuary," "Pirates."

Hither to uncollected fiction:

The Flint Knige, Wellington, Northampton Shire: Equation, 1988. Selected and introduced by Jack Adrian. Contains "The Flint Knife," "The Chippendale Mirror," "Witch-Ball," "The Ape," "Sir Roger de Coverly," "The China Bowl," The Passenger," "The Friend in the Garden," "The Red House," "'Through'", "The Box at the Bank," "The Light in the Garden," "Dummy on a Dahabeah," "The Return of Frank Hampden," "The Shuttered Room."

Novels
The Judgment Books, London: Osgood, McIlvaine, 1895.
The Luck of the Vails, London: Heinemann, 1901.
The Image in the Sand, London: William Heinemann, 1905.
The Angel of Pain, Philadelphia: Lippincott, 1905.
David Blaize and the Blue Door, London: Hodder & Stoughton, 1918.
Across the Stream, London: John Murray, 1919.
Colin and *Colin II*, London: Hutchinson, 1923 and 1925.
The Inheritor, London: Hutchinson, 1930.
Raven's Brood, London: Arthur Barker, 1934.

THE SHADOW OVER DERLETH

Paul Spencer

It seems hardly credible that such a giant figure as August Derleth could be lost in another man's shadow. Yet to many of today's readers he is probably known chiefly for founding Arkham House to preserve in book form the writings of H. P. Lovecraft, and for writing new stories in Lovecraft's Cthulhu Mythos cycle. In actuality, of course, Derleth's other accomplishments were manifold — in detective stories, in serious regional fiction and nonfiction, in poetry, and independently in Lovecraft's own field of supernatural horror.

There is a special irony in the fact that Derleth's own weird stories are quite unlike Lovecraft's. The stories that imitate Lovecraft or that evolved out of Lovecraft's notes represent an attempt by Derleth to write in a manner profoundly foreign to him — an attempt that did little justice to either man. In contrast, after a tentative and imitative apprenticeship, Derleth developed a type of supernatural tale that in both manner and content was far more closely allied to the realism of his own "mainstream" work — the "Sac Prairie Saga" — than to the Lovecraft mythos. It was in the best of such stories that Derleth made his real contribution as a writer in what he liked to call "the domain of the macabre."

Indeed, Derleth came comparatively late to the pasticching of Lovecraft. Apart from a 1932 collaboration with Mark Schorer, his first such tale, "The Return of Hastur," was written around 1936; but Derleth's work had been appearing regularly in *Weird Tales* magazine for ten years previous, with no trace of the Lovecraftian. "Hastur" was soon followed by "The Sandwin Compact," and Derleth included both tales in the first Arkham House collection of his own writings, *Someone in the Dark* (1941). His second collection, *Something Near* (1945) included four such narratives. These were followed by the episodic novel *The Trail of Cthulhu* (1962) and the tales collected as *The Mask of Cthulhu* (1958). Examples also appear in his final collection, *Dwellers in Darkness* (1976) and in the Derleth Schorer collaborations, *Colonel Markesan and Less Pleasant People* (1966).

Others among them achieved a special status because they were presented as "by H. P. Lovecraft and August Derleth." While all such stories were based upon notes left by HPL, only "The Survivor" was fully plotted by him. Actual Lovecraft prose appears — in small measure — only in *The Lurker at the Threshold* (1945) and "The Lamp of Alhazred." The collaborative volumes *The Lurker at the Threshold* and *The Survivor and Others* (1957), together with the omnibus collection *The Watchers Out of Time and Others* (1974), may be necessities for the Lovecraft collector, but they are placed more appropriately among the works of Derleth.

In fact, however, they are not at home in the territory of either. Stylistically they attempt to imitate Lovecraft, but they fail to capture his atmospheric rhythms and sonorities. Instead, Derleth borrows the most superficial and often the most regrettable elements of HPL's prose: the long, involved sentences, the intense and often exotic adjectives and adverbs, the revelatory denouements in italic type. The plots are indeed in the Lovecraft mold, but usually too much so — mere variations (though sometimes quite clever ones) on familiar Cthulhoid themes.

Where Derleth introduced novelty into the pastiches, it was in a way that falsified and trivialized the Mythos. For Lovecraft's hints of cosmic chaos, with their disquieting philosophical and psychological implications, he substituted the banality of the traditional struggle between good evil. Further, he reduced Lovecraft's unique ultradimensional entities to elementals of earth, air, fire, and water. He managed this only by adding his own beings to complete the four elements.

Some of the later tales, to be sure — "The Fisherman of Falcon Point, " "Witches' Hollow," "The Shadow in the Attic," "The Dark Brotherhood," "Innsmouth Clay" — do less violence to the Lovecraft tradition, but by moving further away from it. "The Lamp of Alhazred," though, reflects credit upon both men, not merely because of the authentic Lovecraft it contains but because this fantasy is not so much a horror story as a graceful and ingenious tribute to HPL and a moving elegy upon his death.

Even the best of the Lovecraftian tales, however, conceal what Derleth really had to offer the aficionado of the weird. It is further masked by Derleth's own hasty productivity. (Among *Weird Tales* authors only Seabury Quinn could compete with him in sheer volume of output.) Writing for such a low-paying market, and having some much larger literary fish to fry, he could not always take the time to create fresh ideas or to put a high gloss on his work. Yet each Derleth collection contains things that are worth preserving and rereading, and that exemplify the fine work of which he was capable.

Several markedly un-Lovecraftian qualities give these tales their appeal: a clear, cool style, restrained in tone and often elegant in phrasing; an emphasis upon character and psychological insight; ingenuity in twisting familiar supernatural themes into bizarre new shapes; and, frequently, a mordant sense of humor. Indeed, whether he writes of ghosts or demons, monsters or voodoo, only rarely does Derleth set out actually to frighten — though on occasion he does so with memorable success (see "Glory Hand" in *Someone in the Dark* or "The Satin Mask" in *Something Near*).

More often, his tales amuse in a sardonic way, or else they evoke a sense of compassion for lonely, thwarted people or provide the satisfaction of seeing unadmirable persons meet appropriately ghastly ends. In contrast to the inescapable dooms that befall Lovecraft's innocent seekers after truth, the fate of Derleth's protagonists is exactly what they deserve, for better or worse. Thus the supernatural element is not simply imposed upon the leading characters but is a symbolic expression of their psyches. In aim and sometimes in accomplishment, such stories are less akin to the pulp thrillers of magazines like *Weird Tales* than to the literate and sensitive storytelling of British masters such as M. R. James, Algernon Blackwood, H. R. Wakefield, and L. P. Hartley. Among Americans, one thinks of Mary Wilkins-Freeman, Edith Wharton, and Henry James.

Moreover, in the course of Derleth's career the proportion of outstanding work increased. To be sure, some fine, uniquely Derlethian tales were first published as far back as the early 1930's, and were included in the first three collections, *Someone in the Dark*, *Something Near*, and the 1948 *Not Long for This World*. Among the always entertaining but sometimes bland stories in these books are several charming, character-centered dark comedies. These are written in a tone of playful malice and usually conclude with a particularly telling bit of irony, as in "A Gift for Uncle Herman," "After You, Mr. Henderson," or "Headlines for Tod Shayne." Some of the serious tales, however, indicate more clearly the line of development Derleth was to follow.

As far back as 1930, at age 21, Derleth demonstrated in "The Lilac Bush" his ability to tell a quiet, understated little narrative, free of rhetorical embellishments but powerful in its psychological implications. Like "Nellie Foster" and "Wild Grapes," it reminds one that at the same time he was making his early contributions to *Weird Tales* Derleth was sharpening his skills as a writer of realistic stories for the literary journals.

In "The Shuttered House" he shows a more fully developed ability to blend the horror of the supernatural with that of psychological sickness. Better yet is "The Panelled Room," perhaps Derleth's most successful weird and surely a classic in the field. Not only is the suspense artfully created and intensified, but at the end the menace of the haunted parlor is surpassed by the horror of Irma's psychotic reaction to it. Here, as in such other Thirties tales as "The Sheraton Mirror" and "The·Wind from the River," the uncanny emerges with chilling fatefulness from the interactions of believable people.

It was in the 1940's and 1950's, however, that Derleth matured as a writer of weird fiction. This is shown by the high percentage of original and impressive work from this period in *Lonesome Places* (1962) and *Mr. George and Other Odd Persons* (1963). Appropriately, the stories in the latter — his best collection — were published under the pseudonym of Stephen Grendon, the name of the autobiographical character in the Sac Prairie Saga. For in many of them the contributor to *Weird Tales* merges with the mainstream author. (This development is illustrated in reverse by the inclusion of two supernatural novelettes, "Where the Worm Dieth Not" and "One Against the Dead," in Derleth's otherwise realistic *Sac Prairie People*.)

In the story "Mr. George" itself, for example, the working out of a vengeance from beyond the grave is given conviction by the matter-of-factness of the style, and still more by the vivid characterizations, the realistic texture of the background, and the touching depiction of the relationship between a child and her father, which continues even when he is dead.

In another story in this volume, "The Man on B-17," the link to Derleth's more traditionally literary work is quite specific. It is not merely that there is persuasive use of realistic description and characterization: the story is actually an expanded version of three poems in the "Sac Prairie People" section of Derleth's *Collected Poems*: "Ted Birkett," "Bart Hinch," and "Lois Malone" — poems obviously based on real persons and events. And Derleth's intimate knowledge of his beloved Wisconsin countryside lends depth and a sense of verity even to such modest regional tales as "Parrington's Pool" and "Dead Man's Shoes."

The hand of the author of the Sac Prairie Saga is also apparent in "Mara" and "Alannah." In these highly atmospheric stories lonely people find in the paranormal not retribution but solace, and the emotional impact is impressive. Even the selections that follow the same pattern as the early comedies of doom are written with greater refinement and a more genuine sense of menace — "A Gentleman from Prague," "The Extra Passenger," "The Blue Spectacles," and especially the memorable "Mrs. Manifold."

In *Lonesome Places,* perhaps the finest piece is "The Dark Boy." The earlier Derleth would probably have used as the climax the fact that the extra child in the classroom is a ghost. Here, however, it is simply one step towards a denouement that is far more meaningful in human terms, and far more affecting. The simplicity of the narration — sparing in adjectives and adverbs, rich in convincing detail — supports the believability of the emotional content. similar economy of style adds to the effectiveness of such diverse tales in this collection as the surprising "Hector" and the grotesque "Sexton, Sexton on the Wall."

Even in this mature volume there are lapses into bombastic attempts at Lovecraftian sonorities, as in "The Slayers and the Slain." Yet at times — in "The Lonesome Place," for example — Derleth also demonstrates that he can be a poet in prose as well as in verse, evoking mood with the sound of words and the rhythms of his sentences, in a manner quite his own.

The increasing number of polished and quietly powerful stories in Derleth's later output makes one regret that after the demise of *Weird Tales* in 1954 he concentrated on exploiting the Cthulhu Mythos. Still, his finest fantasies remain as evidence that the Lovecraftian and the prolific pulp writer was also the man whose literary skills and human insight created major contributions to American regional literature. "The Panelled Room," "The Dark Boy," "Mr. George," and other examples of the best Derleth prove that an evocative simplicity is well able to communicate the uncanny; they affirm that humor, compassion, and psychological realism have their place in weird fiction.

It may well be, then, that as anthologists discover and preserve the stories in which Derleth is most truly himself, he will emerge from Lovecraft's shadow and win his own place in the sun as, at times, a particularly sensitive craftsman of the macabre.

BIBLIOGRAPHY

by August Derleth:

Someone in the Dark. Sauk City, Wisc.: Arkham House, 1941. Paperback edition, New York, N.Y.: Jove Publications, 1978.

Something Near. Sauk City, Wisc.: Arkham House, 1945

Not Long for This World. Sauk City, Wisc.: Arkham House, 1948. Paperback edition, New York, N.Y.: Ballantine Books, 1961 (contains 22 of the 32 stories in the hardcover edition).

Sac Prairie People. Sauk City, Wisc.: Stanton and Lee, 1948.

The Mask of Cthulhu. Sauk City, Wisc.: Arkham House, 1958. Paperback edition, New York, N.Y.: Beagle Books, 1971.

Lonesome Places. Sauk City, Wisc.: Arkham House, 1962.

The Trail of Cthulhu. Sauk City, Wisc.: Arkham House, 1962.

Collected Poems. New York, N.Y.: Candlelight Press, 1967.

Dwellers in Darkness. Sauk City, Wisc.: Arkham House, 1976.

by "Stephen Grendon":

Mr. George and Other Odd Persons. Sauk City, Wisc.: Arkham House, 1963. Paperback edition, New York, N.Y.: Belmont Books, 1964.

by H. P. Lovecraft and August Derleth:

The Lurker at the Threshold. Sauk City, Wisc.: Arkham House, 1945. Paperback edition, New York, N.Y.: Beagle Books, 1971 (also Ballantine Books, New York, 1976).

The Survivor and Others. Sauk City, Wisc.: Arkham House, 1957. Paperback edition, New York, N.Y.: Ballantine Books, 1972.

The Watchers Out of Time and Others. Sauk City, Wisc.: Arkham House, 1974.

by August Derleth and Mark Schorer:

Colonel Markesan and Less Pleasant People. Sauk City, Wisc.: Arkham House, 1966.

OLIVER ONIONS:
The Man at the Edge

Mike Ashley

When considering the truly classic tales of the supernatural - stories like "The White People" by Arthur Machen, "The Willows" by Algernon Blackwood, "The Turn of the Screw" by Henry James —there is one that will almost certainly always make the final list: "The Beckoning Fair One" by Oliver Onions. Robert Aickman regarded it as "one of the (possibly) six great masterpieces in the field," believing that it is "an almost perfect story". Jack Sullivan has called it "one of the most beautifully written ghost stories in English" to which Everett Bleiler has added, "...in the opinion of many, the best classical ghost story."

Yet whilst much has been written about Machen, Blackwood and James, little has been written about Oliver Onions, and it even requires a degree of prompting to even remember him when discussing classic horror writers. Apart from "The Beckoning Fair One", and possibly "Phantas," his stories are seldom reprinted and most of his work has long been out of print. It is time for a reappraisal of one of the field's truly unique talents.

The author of "The Beckoning Fair One" was a Yorkshireman, born in Bradford on July 29, 1873. His full name was George Oliver Onions and it was later changed by deed poll to George Oliver, but the name Oliver Onions was retained for all of his writing. He had all the grit, belligerence and determination that is associated with those from the land of the three Ridings (Bradford was also the birthplace of Cutcliffe Hyne and J.B. Priestley, both of similar ilk). From the age of fourteen, his ambition was to illustrate books. In 1894 he earned a scholarship to London, for three years, studying at the National Arts Training School, spending another year in Paris. During this period he wrote his first story, "Smoking Flax", published in the *Lady's Pictorial*, but he had no serious literary inclination. Back in London in 1898 he secured work as a draughtsman, illustrating posters, books and magazines. Even in those days, the threat of the camera and the improved rotary press, was taking its toll. "If I remember rightly, seven of us hit the pavement one week," he later reminisced.

By then, though, he had written his first book. Having been asked by Gelett Burgess to pass an opinion on one of his stories, and having replied with natural Yorkshire bluntness, Onions found himself challenged to try and do better. The result was *The Compleat Bachelor* (John Murray, 1900), which, through Burgess's intervention, was serialized first in *Harper's Bazaar*. America can thus lay claim to having discovered Onions. With the income from his illustrations dwindling and that from his writing increasing, Onions realized where his future lay. "We do not need two baskets when we have only one egg," he wrote, somewhat self-deprecatingly.

There followed in rapid succession a number of novels and story collections, none of them supernatural, but all of them imbued with a strangeness that became Onions's trademark. He strove always to be different, to establish a style and technique that was individual. His stories were frequently grim and humorless, some bitingly satirical, but always hauntingly real. Onions portrayed the world with nothing masked by veils of pretence. He could never understand why the stories and novels of his wife, Berta Ruck, with all their rose-tinted romanticism, sold so well. Hers was the work of a story-teller, plain and simple. Onions created his stories as he would a painting, with different layers and tones, subtle hints and shades. The results set into a distorted perspective the dichotomies and disturbances of the real world.

Onions' world was steeped in reality; his no-nonsense Yorkshire background having no truck with the supernatural. It was this attitude that, paradoxically, gave strength to his ghost stories, making them as disturbingly real as your own inner doubts and worries. As Onions later recorded, what he set out to do in his ghost stories was "to investigate...the varying densities of the ghostliness that is revealed when this surface of life, accepted for everyday purposes as stable, is jarred, and for the time of an experience does not recover its equilibrium."

It was Berta Ruck who directly inspired "The Beckoning Fair One" by jarring Onions momentarily out of his equilibrium. It was shortly after their marriage, when they were living in a dark old house in New End Square, Hampstead. One winter's night Berta was combing her long hair, the coldness of the air increasing the static. Onions, who was already in bed, looked up. "There is no sound that can be mistaken for the crackling of a woman's long hair under the comb," he remarked and then, suddenly captured by the thought, he added: "Imagine if one heard that sound without seeing any woman standing there."

That was the catalyst. When Onions had completed the story and read it to his wife, it scared her witless. In fact she never allowed him to read the end. For her the house was now permanently haunted and at length they were compelled to move. "The Beckoning Fair One" is a long story, Onions taking the time to remove the layers of reality. Paul Oleron, a writer, has rented some rooms in the hope to completing his novel *Romilly Bishop*, but he finds it hard to concentrate. Despite the urgings of his friend, Elsie Bengough, Oleron starts to withdraw both mentally and physically from company. Elsie senses a rejection, not just from Oleron, but from the rooms themselves, which gradually possess Oleron. There are no overt spectral manifestations; simply the hint of an old folk tune, called "The Beckoning Fair One," suggested by the dripping of a tap and, later, only after Oleron has begun his mental disintegration, the crackling of a lady's hair under the comb.

At this point in the story Onions states simply but effectively the rational basis for the irrational, merging in one sudden moment of awareness the real with the unreal:

> Formerly, Oleron had smiled at the fantastic thought that, by a merging and interplay of identities between himself and his beautiful room, he might be preparing a ghost for the future; it had not occurred to him that there might have been a similar merging and coalescence in the past.

"The Beckoning Fair One" was published in Onions's first collection of ghost stories, most aptly entitled *Widdershins* (1911). He had two other original volumes, *Ghosts in Daylight* (1924) and *The Painted Face* (1929), plus the omnibus *Collected Ghost Stories* (1935) which contained all that Onions cared to collect, and from which was selected the delightfully entitled *Bells Rung Backwards* (1953). In total he completed some twenty-four strange stories, almost all of them worthy of attention, and a few almost the equal of "The Beckoning Fair One".

"The Painted Face," a short novel in its own right, may at length be regarded as one of the finest works in the genre. It tells of a young girl, Xena Francavilla, who is by nature shy and withdrawn. She joins a party of girls chaperoned by and English lady, travelling to Tunisia. Here Xena suddenly comes alive, fired to some extent by a renewed acquaintance with an Englishman, Verney Arden. Some of Xena's true personality is gradually revealed: it seems she is a condemned spirit, cursed from a former existence to be a temptress who will never find love. The strength of the story lies again in character study but this time, instead of mental disintegration, as with Oleron, it is a spiritual re-awakening and the discovery of fate. "The Painted Face" does not have the haunting uncertainty of "The Beckoning Fair One," but has instead an unsettling mysteriousness, much of Xena's nature only being determined from half-understood events and disjointed incidents. Like "The Beckoning Fair One", "The Painted Face" is a masterpiece of construction.

Onion did not always require the novella-length to develop his situations—in fact some stories, like "The Rosewood Door" and "The Real People" suffer from their length, being unnecessarily verbose. A handful of short stories, however, have an almost equal impact. Of these, perhaps the best in their unrelenting strangeness are "Rooum" and "Benlian". Drawing on his artistic youth, Onions made "Benlian" the artist's fantasy. Benlian is a sculptor who has created a hideous stone statue which he regards as his god and to which he seeks to transfer his personality. The story is narrated by a painter who serves as a witness to the events and who narrates them from an asylum. "Rooum" has similar hints of madness. Rooum is the name given to a transient engineer with intuitive skills who is plagued by something unseen which he claims pursues him and even runs "through" him. The story develops rapidly as Rooum endeavors to kill the "runner" only to meet an inevitable fate.

Fate, and a merging of the past and future, is a frequent theme in Onions's stories. In "Phantas," a dying Elizabethan sailor has a vision of a ship of the future and the vision becomes a reality. In "The Accident" Romarin has a vision of events leading to murder and by his own action avoids that train of events. "The Ascending Dram" looks at the evolution of attainment over successive eras, whilst "The Cigarette Case," "The Rosewood Door," and "John Gladwyn Says..." are all studies in time dislocation.

Only one of Onions's stories is based on a real supernatural incident, which happened to his elder son Arthur. Arthur was studying for his exams and rented a hotel room with a fellow student. During the first night the friend awoke hearing someone pacing about the room. He thought at first it was Arthur until he found Arthur was still asleep. Later that night Arthur awoke and had the same experience. Over the next few days they grew more acutely aware of this presence which they could not see but could hear, could feel by a sudden coldness and which smelt of damp earth. This incident was too good for Onions to ignore and he used it as a central part to "The Rope in the Rafters" about a man, disfigured during the First World War, who becomes the victim of supernatural events at an old French chateau.

Onions is justifiably remembered for his short stories but today most of his novels are unfairly neglected, even his masterwork — the murder trilogy which began with *In Accordance With the Evidence* (1912) — is drifting into obscurity. In his day some of his novels were critically acclaimed whilst others suffered too much from his untraditional approach. Few have any supernatural association but a number share that same dislocation of reality as his shorter works. One of the earliest was *The Tower of Oblivion* (1921), a bold attempt at another character study, this time of a man, Derwent Rose, who is driven to the conclusion that at one point in his life his personal time reversed and he is now growing younger in periodic leaps, with the prospect of dying at sixteen. The novel is perhaps overlong, and fails to totally involve the reader, although it does have some powerful and some poignant passages as Rose's fate draws near.

One of the strangest of Onions's novels is *The Hand of Kornelius Voyt* (1939), a disquieting story of isolation and alienation. It tells of young Peter Byles, orphaned and separated from his sister, who comes into the house of Dr. Voyt to be tutored by the enigmatic Heinrich Opfer. As the story develops Peter finds himself increasingly alienated from Opfer while becoming psychically attracted to Voyt, whom he seldom sees. Onions does little to help the reader understand the unreality of the situation which is tangible in its desolation, and which remains unresolved at its conclusion.

In a sense, alienation is the driving force of much of Onions's work. Perhaps he felt isolated and removed from society. Certainly he strove to be unorthodox, often to the detriment of his reputation. As the years took their toll Onions also felt increasingly isolated from the twentieth century, feeling a closer affinity with the past. This sense of dislocation and rejection reached its peak n what some regard as his best work, *The Story of Ragged Robyn* (1945). It is ostensibly a historical novel, set in the seventeenth century in the unclaimed marshes of Loncolnshire, but it's a world created with such a sense of distorted reality that it might as well be a fantasy milieu. Sir John Betjeman said of it that "such a feeling of remoteness, boding inevitability, horror, such a sense of the past and such narrative power are rarely found in one book." Young Robyn Skyrme incurs the wrath of local bandits who vow they will exact terrible vengeance in seven years' time. Robyn runs away and has a series of strange experiences as an apprentice stonemason before the seven years is over and he finds himself on trial by the bandits for his past misdemeanors. It is poetically written with a touching finale.

Few writers in the field come close to Onions in evoking that unsettling feeling of isolation, alienation and remoteness, and in creating an atmosphere of total strangeness. Perhaps his successor in the realms of the weird was Robert Aickman, but Onions's development of this obsession went beyond his "ghost" stories to historical, sociological and psychological dramatic studies.

Onions died on April 9, 1961, aged 87. An unfinished fantasy, *A Shilling to Spend*, was published posthumously in 1965. It is uncharacteristically light-hearted and undeserving as a swan-song. Onions had a rare talent, and one not to be treated lightly.

BIBLIOGRAPHY

This bibliography is limited to Onions's works of supernatural or fantastic fiction and associated items cited above.

Short Fiction

Widdershins, London: Martin Secker, 1911. Contains "The Beckoning Fair One," "Phantas," "Rooum," "Benlian," "Io," "The Accident," "The Cigarette Case," "The Rocker," and "Hic Jacet". Note that "The Rocker" was omitted from the 1925 reprinting (London: Adelphi) and from most subsequent reprintings.

Ghosts in Daylight, London: Chapman & Hall, 1924. Contains "The Ascending Dream," "The Honey in the Wall," "The Dear Dryad," "The Real People," and "The Woman in the Way."

The Painted Face, London: William Heinemann, 1929. Contains "The Painted Face," "The Rosewood Door," and "The Master of the House."

The Collected Ghost Stories, London: Ivor Nicholson & Watson, 1935. Omnibus of the above three volumes but omitting "The Rocker" and "Dear Dryad" and adding "The Out Sister," "John Gladwyn Says," "The Rope in the Rafters," and "Resurrection in Bronze."

Bells Rung Backward, London: Staples Press, 1953. Retrospective collection containing "The Rosewood Door," "The Woman in the Way," "The Honey in the Wall," "John Gladwyn Says," and "The Painted Face."

Uncollected stories are:

"The Mortal" and "The Ether Hogs" both in *The Ghost Book* edited by Cynthia Asquith, London: Hutchinson, 1926.
"The Smile of Karen" in *The Black Cap* edited by Cynthia Asquith, London: Hutchinson, 1927.

Novels
The New Moon, London: Hodder & Stoughton, 1918.
The Tower of Oblivion, London: Hodder & Stoughton, 1921.
A Certain Man, London: William Heinemann, 1931.
The Hand of Kornelius Voyt, London: Chapman & Hall, 1939.
The Story of Ragged Robyn, London: Michael Joseph, 1945.
A Shilling to Spend, London: Michael Joseph, 1965.

W. C. MORROW:

Forgotten Master of Horror—The First Phase

Sam Moskowitz

Long-lasting literary fame is rarely established without the permanence of a hard-cover volume. A masterpiece may appear in a publication of a million circulation, but it has a better chance of surviving if it is published in a book, even if only in a 1,000-copy print order. Books are kept, catalogued and reviewed. Books are borrowed from public libraries and read; they may catch the eye in a casual perusal of the stacks and be read. Magazines, even when kept by libraries, are held in the reference sections and are catalogued by date and volume number and are not readily available.

The only reason the name of William Chambers Morrow (1854-1923) still endures can be credited to one superbly crafted volume containing 14 of his magazine stories collected under the title of *The Ape The Idiot & Other People* by Lippincott in 1897. It was reprinted in England in 1898 by Grant Richards and in France in 1901 as *Le Singe L'Idiot et Autres Gens* by Editions de la Revue Blanche, Paris. From this volume, magazines—*Weird Tales* and *Golden Book* among them—reprinted an occasional story and anthologists have made selections, right up to this very day. What is not generally known is that a number of his stories were printed abroad as pick-up from various American periodicals received there (the reverse was also a common practice in the United States), including stories that had never been collected in the book! Additionally, several straight science fiction pieces by Morrow, which never appeared in the United States, were published in England at least.

One story of his, "The Three Hundred" (*The Argonaut,* January 10, 1880), was dramatized as a thirty-minute television show in the fifties, though no further printing since its first has yet been uncovered. (It either was picked up from some unlocated anthology, plagiarized, or is actually based on a true, repeatable incident.

Previous to this, the most comprehensive review of Morrow's life and works appeared in *Science Fiction in Old San Francisco: Volume I, History of the Movement from 1854 to 1890* by Sam Moskowitz (Donald M. Grant, Providence, 1980) and his career will be substantially added to when the second volume of the history is

. published. When one realizes that no bibliography of first publication of the works of Ambrose Bierce has ever been compiled, let alone those of William Morrow, it can be seen how easily the impression arises that the latter was powerfully influenced by the former, whereas in actuality the *reverse* was the case. There seems little doubt that the single major influence on the short stories of Ambrose Bierce was William Morrow. But in order to establish that, it is necessary to establish the chronological first publication of the works of each, supplemented by knowledge of their personal relationship and views of one another.

Therefore, when the much-loved critic Vincent Starrett in his book *Buried Caesars* (Covici-McGee Co., Chicago, 1923) set out to do justice to outstanding literary figures he felt he had been ignored (Ambrose Bierce and Arthur Machen were among those included), he also had a short chapter on "The Art of W. C. Morrow." He could think of no higher praise than to say that Morrow's stories "might also have been written by Ambrose Bierce, whose method—a singularly effective one—was to seize the bare facts of a tragedy at the moment of its supreme emotion, and from that point present them stripped of explanatory influences." What he didn't know was that the method he described was employed as a standard procedure in almost all of Morrow's stories at a time when Bierce had only one or two works of fiction published. That further, Ambrose Bierce was well acquainted with Morrow in that early period when he was writing no fiction on his own, because he was editor of *The Argonaut*, a leading San Francisco weekly, and in that capacity bought at least the first seven and possibly the first ten of Morrow's stories himself! And all of those stories were just as Starrett described them. Morrow never changed; Bierce did not become a success in fiction until he adopted Morrow's methods!

"Having named Poe and Bierce," Starrett continued, "one must turn to France and Guy de Maupassant for the third and only other man in modern letters whose urge may have gone into the making of W. C. Morrow." This would have been more convincing if he had been aware that Morrow had seven stories published in *The Argonaut* in 1879, the year before Maupassant scored the first short story success of his life with "Boule de Suif," a tale of prostitute and members of the upper classes together on the road during the invasion of France, which first appeared in a volume of new stories by six French authors, *Soirées de Médan*. This book attracted attention because it was edited and with an introduction by Emile Zola and also included Paul Alexis, Henry Ceard, J. K. Huysmans and Leon Hennique as well as de Maupassant. The book appeared April 17, 1880 and since Maupassant was literally unknown to the French public, let alone to Americans, he could scarcely have been an important influence on Morrow at that period.

Edgar Allan Poe was, of course, an influence—strangely enough—on Morrow's detective stories. Therefore we find Morrow writing detective stories very like those of A. Conan Doyle, seven to eight years before the latter ever published Sherlock Holmes!

It is a common practice for critics to accept book publication as first publication. This is often true in the case of novels but less frequently in the case of collections of short stories. The notion that Bierce was an influence on Morrow rests on the fact that two collections of Bierce's stories preceded *The Ape The Idiot & Other People*, *Tales of Soldiers*, (1891), and *Can Such Things Be?* (1893).

The truth was that Ambrose Bierce produced a minimal amount of fiction until he was hired on a salary basis ($35 a week to start) by William Randolph Hearst to write his column "Prattle" for *The San Francisco Examiner*. Bierce did not begin producing fiction again until 1888 and then infrequently, while W. C. Morrow was already contributing his power-house stories to the *Examiner* in 1887 and that year returned to *The Argonaut* with "The Surgeon's Experiment," published in revised form in his book as "The Monster Maker." This would be followed by some of his very finest work within the following two years. It was almost immediately following this that Bierce began producing the superb stories that would be quickly collected in *Tales of Soldiers and Civilians*.

Not only had the men known each other since Bierce bought Morrow's early stories in 1879, but they had debated back and forth in the columns of *The San Francisco Examiner*. In his April 1, 1888, colum "Prattle," Bierce devoted a portion to advertising Morrow's brilliance, stating in reference to that author's novel *Blood-Money:* "I know nothing in literature surpassing the ghastly realism of Mr. Morrow's manner in depicting with minute peculiarity the progressive stages of this horrible surgical operation (amputating one's own leg)....It is really one of the most powerful studies in that kind of art ever executed in words."

This, despite the fact that Morrow in a lengthy letter in the February 26 *Examiner* headed "Reporter's English," had taken Bierce to task for his grammar and punctuation (Morrow was considered expert in this regard, writing a book which was published posthumously as *The Logic of Punctuation for All Who Have to do With Written English,* published by H. Low, San Francisco, in 1926.) Bierce, famous for his scathing retorts, took Morrow to heart and replied carefully and respectfully, and with some justice, on his own views on grammar and punctuation in the March 4, 1886 edition of *The Examiner.*

Guillaume Apollinaire, the famed French avant-garde artist and author (1880-1918), made the claim that the title of H. G. Wells' *The Island of Dr. Moreau* (1896) was taken by converting Morrow's anglicized name to its original French "Moreau"—reflecting Wells' admiration for Morrow's "The Monster Maker." It was pointed out, in refutation, that Morrow's collection had not appeared, even in the United States, until one year after Wells' work. Those critics were not aware that the original title of "The Monster Maker" had been "The Scientist's Experiment" and that it was originally published in 1887. *The Argonaut,* the magazine in which it was published, had good London circulation and its original stories were frequently pirated by British magazines and newspapers. In simply checking a single year of the British weekly *Short Stories* (a companion to *Pearson's Magazine* and *Pearson's Weekly),* twenty positive identifications of stories reprinted from *The Argonaut* were made. (This check was primarily in regard to fantasies; it was not practical to check every story, since the selections were chosen over a ten-year range!) This does not include stories for which the title, byline, or both were changed! Now it so happens that in 1896 Wells' *The War of the Worlds,* along with some of his short stories, was running in *Pearson's Magazine* and in 1897 his *The Invisible Man* would be serialized in *Pearson's Weekly.* It also happens that Morrow's "The Scientist's Experiment" was reprinted anonymously in *Pearson's Weekly* in the issue of April 11, 1896. Since the book publication of Wells' *The Island of Dr. Moreau* was in March, 1896, *that* printing could not have influenced him. However, since Morrow's story was already nine years old, there had probably been previous piratings of it. In that one year of *Short Stories,* there were *two* stories by Morrow among the contents. Neither story has ever been collected in book form.

The moral of the foregoing paragraph is that the date of published books is not a reliable method of establishing or disproving literary theories. Book dates seem to prove Apollinaire's theory about H. G. Wells' linkage with Morrow to be wrong. Magazine publication dates and publishing practices of the period give him the benefit of a doubt.

Further, the foregoing also indicates that Morrow is an author worth examining, if influence is a criterion by which worth may be judged. To better appreciate and evaluate Morrow's fiction, an examination of what facts are known about his early background is important. Particularly so since Morrow was born in Selma, Alabama (the *deepest* South before the Civil War) on July 7, 1854. His male relatives fought on the Southern side and there are indications in at least one of this stories that he may have been training at a military school when the war ended. The records show that he was a slave holder at the age of five: two slaves, a 33-year-old female and a 19-year-old male being registered in his name. His father, also named William Chambers, owned two additonal slaves: a female aged 25 and a male aged 5. The relatives on his mother's side owned, among them, 172 slaves! Why two slaves were registered in Junior's name as early as 1860 can only be surmised. Perhaps they were a legacy or a birth gift as the first family male, possibly made by a slave-rich relative of his mother. Perhaps there was a legal technicality that made it financially advisable to have the family credit several slaves to the name of their son.

Morrow's first nine published stories, though written in San José, California, all have Southern backgrounds and have free and slave Negroes, moonshiners, Southern soldiers, and Southern entertainers as protagonists. They are a valuable literary record of the attitudes of a young Southerner towards slavery and the Civil War, written only a decade after that era in the history of the United States had ended. From his first to his last story, the shock of physical and psychological horror was omnipresent in all but a few. He gradually moved from writing primarily horror into supernatural, detective, and science fiction as well. One of his earliest efforts at science fiction involved two Negro slaves.

Morrow's father was a Baptist minister, born June 6, 1815 in Pulaski County, Tennessee. He moved to Alabama as a boy and prepared for the Presbyterian ministry while still in his teens. He left the Presbyterian church for the Baptist in 1841 and took charge of a congregation in Turnbull, Monroe County, Alabama. He married Martha Ann McCreary on June 24, 1844. She was only 14, some 15 years younger than he. The reason for her youthful marriage seems to have been the death of her parents, as they were not listed among the living in the census of 1850. By that year the couple already had two children, both girls: Sarah, aged five and Georgiana, aged two. Another daughter, Mary, was born in 1853, to be followed by William, Jr. in 1854. Another brother and sister, Lorenzo and Martha, were born in the sixties, but apparently these two died before the census of 1870 was taken. There would be a last girl, Danzilla.

In 1850 the elder Morrow's family was living in Conecuh County, Alabama, with property valued at $400. By 1860 the father was listed as a member of the clergy with real property worth $1,280 and personal property valued at $4,615. The last figure may have included the value of his four slaves.

In 1869 the elder Morrow became too ill to continue his ministry, though the 1870 census lists a hotel among the family assets in Evergreen, Alabama, valued at $3,000. Personal property is estimated at only $700, indicating that with the termination of the Civil War the slaves had been freed. The hotel business was obviously something he took up as an alternative to the ministry and the burden of the work fell on his wife, daughter Georgiana, and William, Jr. The father had pastored at Belleville Church and Evergreen Baptist Church in Evergreen, Alabama.

The boy had been attending college in Birmingham at a very youthful age. The records of Howard College indicate that he graduated there in 1869. (Since then, the name of the college has been changed to Samford University.)

For lack of other evidence it must be assumed that William Junior helped the family in the hotel during most of the decade of the seventies. The following notice ran in *The Alabama Baptist* for January 2, 1876: "This hotel (Gulf City, Conti and Water Streets, Mobile, Alabama) now under the charge of W. C. Morrow, Jr., formerly a student at Howard College, will be found an agreeable home to the stranger in Mobile. It is very convenient to the railroads, street cars, and commercial houses of the city. The dining room is under the direct supervision of the gentlemanly proprietor. The table is tempting to the dullest appetite. The servants are prompt and polite. The accomplished mother and sisters of Mr. Morrow will see to it that ladies visiting the hotel shall have a pleasant time."

A photo of the hotel, which was relatively new when Morrow took it over, having been erected in 1868, appeared in *Port City*, Mobile, Alabama, August 1, 1982. It was almost a block in length, three stories high, with cast-iron grilled porches on the upper two floors similar to the buildings in New Orleans' French Quarter. The photo, taken in the 20's, depicted quite an impressive structure. The destruction of this hotel started a historic preservation movement in Mobile to halt the elimination of landmark structures. How the Morrows could have afforded to operate so substantial a business is a mystery. It may be deduced that they could not for keep it going for long, as the November 2, 1878 issue of *The Alabama Baptist* carried the notice: "W.C. Morrow, Jr., formerly of the Gulf City Hotel of Mobile, has opened a hotel in Meridian, Mississippi. We could only advise anyone who may visit Meridian to put up at Morrow's Hotel. Mr. Morrow knows how to make guests comfortable and will do so." Meridian is a small city about 110 miles northwest of Mobile, near the Alabama border.

The father died in October, 1879 and it was earlier that year that the younger Morrow, at the age of twenty-five, had left the family for California. His mother and sisters presumably supported themselves by operating some hotel or boarding house. Somewhere in the period between 1869 and 1879 Morrow had also attended the University of Alabama at Tuscaloosa. He was then about six feet tall and starvingly thin, though not emaciated, with blond hair. In later years he filled out and cultivated a full mustache extending the length of his upper lip, setting off a rather handsome face with a scholarly expression.

There are difficult-to-fill gaps in the life of William C. Morrow, Jr. It was said that his college and university instructors were amazed at his precocious writing ability, yet there is no record that anything was ever published while he lived in Alabama. When he arrived in Oakland, California, he found only short-lived positions on local newspapers. He obviously had a good education, but for a newpaper position in those days, was a college degree acceptable in lieu of experience? Did he have some material published earlier that might have served as credentials?

One thing is certain. In 1879 W. C. Morrow had written short stories to offer for sale, some of them superior to anything written by anyone on the West Coast that year, and such ability rarely emerges spontaneously. While working for newspapers Morrow met E. H. Clough, who was selling some very well-written and authentic stories with western settings—mining, ranching, pioneer settlements—to a weekly cultural and political publication titled *The Argonaut*. That periodical had been launched in 1877 by two San Francisco newspapermen, Frank Pixley and Fred Somers, who felt there was room for a magazine featuring fiction, poetry, humor, the stage, gossip, political opinion, and literary reviews. They turned out to be right. To help them fulfill their concept, they hired Ambrose Bierce out of the United States San Francisco Mint. Clough took Morrow in hand and personally escorted him to the offices of *The Argonaut* in San Francisco and introduced him to Fred Somers and Ambrose Bierce.

Somers and Bierce were amazed by the tremendous wallop this "beginning" writer packed into his short stories, which contained graphic characterization (unusual in a short story at any time), vivid impact, atmosphere, authentic local color, surprise endings, and a pervasive sense of horror, even in the portrayal of seemingly ordinary events of life. Bierce was especially impressed, for though he had shown excellent critical and satirical ability as a columnist and essayist, wrote tolerable poetry and even did some illustrating, he had not—up to that time—written any fiction comparable to what Morrow was offering for publication.

The first story published (and the earliest so far discovered for Morrow) was "Punishing a Slacker," subtitled "an episode of Southern life." This was not so much a story as a vignette, set against the background of the building of a railroad in the South. Its chief characters are Negro laborers, who discover among their group what they termed a "slacker" by the name of Yaller Tom. A "slacker" is a fellow who plays every angle for shoving off his work on his fellows and doing as little as possible himself.

The word is passed around. Suddenly Yaller Tom finds himself in the grip of six muscular workers. He is strung up on a tree by his ankles, head downward, his hands tied to two stakes on the ground about four feet apart. His pants are removed so that his rear end is naturally air cooled. Then the most powerful of the laborers hefts a board about four feet long, four inches wide and an inch thick and administers twenty tremendous whacks, while a counter marks them off. Another niche is notched in the board and it is put back in its place of honor for future use, as the cured slacker is cut down and released.

There was no question that Morrow could write, but it was the second story, "Awful Shadows," printed in the July 19, 1879 issue, that really displayed his literary skills, as well as elements that were later to be found in many of Ambrose Bierce's stories. "Awful Shadows" opened with the lines: "A crime has been committed in Mississippi. One lovely evening in May, as rosy twilight was stealing on, a little girl dragged herself to her mother's door." The child dies from the savage damage of rape. The atmosphere of fear and hate that hovers over the homes in this Southern town is frighteningly conveyed by Morrow. To these people, this crime is the depth of depravity and inhumanity. Cordons of men mounted and on foot scour the countryside. In the morning they bring in a Negro. The evidence that he is the rapist-killer is overwhelming. The men, enraged, decide that a quick lynching would be too kind a punishment.

They turn their man over to Bony, a Negro railroad fireman with tremendously long, powerful arms and short, squat legs. Bony begins to stoke the engine of his locomotive. Hours pass and night falls; the blazing light of the firebox with the shadow of Bony moving in front of it is all that is visible, casting a shadow as of a monstrous demon. Then, etched in black against the fire, this "demon" seems to be lifting a huge board with something strapped to it. "The blazing fire-door light is temporarily blotted out, then suddenly flares brighter than before." Then, "the demon bending over, his great, naked arm stretched across the opening, as if reaching to close the gate. All was darkness again."

The brutality of the crime and the punishment, set against the background of a society just emerging from slavery, and the powerful characterization of Bony combine to etch a tale of horror in which the supernatural would have been superfluous.

But Morrow, this strange and unique writer, could be sentimental about slavery. His "Old Aunt Rachel" (August 16, 1879) personifies every virtue that can be infused into a black slave. Loved by everyone, no matter what their color, she is a genius at herbicidal medicine and the finest nurse in the county. As a young woman she could pick 300 pounds of cotton a day. Her cooking was beyond praise and she spoiled her mistress unashamedly. There was no one she wouldn't help, but the bane of her existence is Jake, a not-too-bright youngster who is always getting into trouble. One day, riding on the back of a bull, he arouses the cattle so they begin goring everything they can reach, including Rachel.

Aside from the unusual character sketch, the irony is that the last thoughts of the dying Rachel are concerned with the beating she is going to administer to Jake. Fundamentally this is a tale of horror, for in loading Rachel with transcendental virtues, the irony of this good woman finally evaluating an act of punishment tempered by mercy, without the realization that she is dying, erases everything but a feeling of numbness and cosmic injustice.

Again, in "The Burning of the College" (September 6, 1879), a character sketch of an old Negro caretaker at a boys' school, perhaps someone taken from life in Morrow's college days, is brilliantly etched, and his heroism in saving two small boys from a fire at the school is posthumously rationalized thus: "The old man was simply a part of the college—one of its vitals—they belonged each to the other; and when one died it was right that the other should also pass away."

This was followed by "Among the Moonshiners" (October 4, 1879), which again is a real horror story without any element of the supernatural. Detectives tracking moonshiners are exposed to gunfire as they climb up to reach the moonshiners' hideout, a cave. The lawmen manage to throw a makeshift bomb into the cave. After the blast "A thing crawled to the opening. A few seconds ago it was a man. It carried something in its left arm—a shattered leg. It held a knife between its teeth and glared at its enemies. It only half glared. A ball was dangling against one cheek, which annoyed it, and it feebly struck at the ball once. Still the ball dangled, and it grasped the offending object, jerked it from the slender thread that held it, and threw it over the precipice. It was an eye. The thing continued to glare at its murderers."

Morrow transforms suspense into horror in "A Night in New Orleans" (November 15, 1879), as he narrates the progress of a tightrope act. As a promotional stunt, a tightrope is stretched between two buildings, and a girl is to walk across at night. She is feeling poorly and not as sure of herself as she normally would have been. Flares help light the rope, and she tortuously makes one crossing safely, then faces about for the return. Halfway back, the flares go out and she cannot see the rope. She has no choice but to proceed. For a few steps she is all right, but then slips to one knee. A moment later she loses the balancing pole. She falls, but catches the rope and is dangling by one hand. Her male partner crawls out on the rope to rescue her, and now the question is whether she can hold on until he gets to her, and when he does—

how do they get down? With a little ingenuity the rescue is effected, but the events of the night are completely harrowing.

Far more grim is "The Bloodhounds" (December 13, 1879), subtitled "A Sombre Incident of the Civil War." A Confederate soldier deserts and heads home to help feed his family. Months later a searching party with bloodhounds locates him. He eludes them and sets off into a nearby swamp. Twelve bloodhounds are after him, including one known as Old Tighe, who usually waits until the younger dogs have exhausted their best efforts before making his play. In a nightmarish two hours, one at a time, the deserter kills eleven of the dogs with nothing but his bare hands and ingenuity. No more dogs attack and, reeling with fatigue and loss of blood, he makes it to a stream, desperately needing water. As he rises, shock and exhaustion cause him to faint. As he lies unconscious on the ground, Old Tighe emerges from the bushes and rips his throat out! The reader is traumatized by the abrupt and unfair end to a gallant man who has made such an heroic and apparently successful bid for his freedom. With this story, Morrow began to build in the shocking surprise endings which were to become his trademark in the years to come.

The advantage Morrow had over most other short story writers was his ability to incorporate elements of characterization, background color, mood, authentic dialogue, and high originality—all within the compass of a short story. Though most of his work was done in the field of horror, he was every bit as good in mainstream areas. "The Three Hundred" (January 10, 1880) is aptly subtitled "A Southern Story of the War." This deserves to be a standard American classic. Possibly a major reason it has not become one is that it favors the Confederacy. In form, writing, and execution it is a literary masterpiece. Five thousand of Sherman's men are sweeping towards the sea. As far as they know, there is no Confederate armed force between them and the Atlantic coast. Abruptly, on the campus of a university, their way is blocked by several hundred seeming dwarfs, armed with rifles and wearing brand-new Confederate uniforms.

After their initial surprise, the Union officers observe that none of the several hundred "dwarfs" are over fourteen years of age. They are children from the military academy. Seventy Union cavalrymen, with drawn swords, charge towards them, depending on fear to scatter the mock soldiers, whose commandant is an old man, evidently an instructor at the academy. The cavalry charge is met by a wall of fire! Many fall, and they retreat without having themselves fired a shot.

The cavalrymen reform for another charge, and gunfire from the men behind them has already killed one child-soldier. The children's commandant is ready to give the order to retreat behind some protecting embankments. He reaches down for a white flag of surrender, but is killed before he get hold of it. Now a uniformed boy steps forward from the ranks, seizes the Confederate flag and, in the face of the charging cavalry, orders his fellows to stand fast. Some do, and another fusillade is fired at the cavalry. But this time the charge is not stopped, and the children retreat to the embankments—all except the one boy who had assumed command, carrying the dead commandant's sword aloft.

Another charge scatters the children—all except their leader. The Union captain demands that he surrender. The boy refuses. He will surrender only to a full colonel, as that is now his own rank.

"And the man lying there?" the captain asks, trying to determine the identity of the old man.

A tear trembled upon the pale cheek of the boy. Less firmly, he answered:

"My father."

There is not a single unneeded word in the story. It is utterly brilliant. It also raises the question as to whether it has been anthologized somewhere and somehow overlooked, for in the late fifties that very story was shown, with considerable effectiveness, as a thirty-minute TV drama. Because no research had then uncovered the fact that it was written by Morrow, he was given no recognition. It *may* be based on a real-life incident, with both Morrow and the television writer deriving information from the same source. Should that be the case, it in no measure reduces Morrow's literary achievement.

Returning to straight horror in "After the Hanging" (March 2, 1880), Morrow proceeds from the base of a public hanging in old Mississippi. A cluster of young boys (four-and-a-half to seven years of age) are watching the hanging. One of them is Tony, a Negro. In discussing the hanging, he boasts that he wouldn't mind being hung—he's not afraid. He's challenged and actually tries it, but falls to the ground. He tries it again, and chokes a bit before the rope breaks a second time. When urged to try it once more, he has had enough. But the other boys, eager to test whether or not hanging hurts, overpower him and hang him from a tree. They don't do it very well, and he thrashes, grimaces, chokes, and finally unable to speak, pleads with his eyes. But they watch dispassionately, almost scientifically.

"We'll take him down after a while," one boy says.

"I'll bet you he won't go around any more blowing about it's not hurting him," another adds.

When he remains perfectly still, they debate whether he is pretending, but they finally cut him down. Only one of the boys understands that Tony is dead. The others, alarmed, "felt that something awful had happened, but they were ignorant of its nature."

From the foregoing group of stories we have evidence of Morrow's extraordinary ability to evoke horror from many a situation which in other hands might be just another piece of realism, regionalism, or adventure.

Study of these stories will reveal that they were the models that Ambrose Bierce later selected when he moved seriously into the writing of short stories. Moreover, some of these stories are easily as good as the best that Bierce ever wrote.

At the end of 1879, Ambrose Bierce resigned as full-time editor of *The Argonaut,* but he continued to do some work and to make occasional contributions into early 1880, when he secured what he thought was a surefire Get-Rich-Quick position in the Black Hills country of North Dakota.

Back at the editorial office, one of the co-owners (Fred Somers) got restless and decided to start a quality monthly West Coast magazine to take the place of the defunct *Overland Monthly.* Among the leading writers for *The Argonaut* were Robert Duncan Milne, who would become the world's first full-time science-fiction writer, penning 60 such tales before his untimely death from an altercation with a cable car in 1899; Emma Frances Dawson, an eccentric recluse and a superb master of the supernatural; and, of course, Ambrose Bierce. Somers got them *all* to contribute to the first issue of his new magazine, *The Californian,* dated January, 1880. He felt that W. C. Morrow belonged with this set of superstars, and so the same issue of the magazine ran "The Man from Georgia," what was later collected in *The Ape The Idiot & Other People* (Lippincott, 1897) as "The Hero of the Plague." This short story caused a minor sensation when it appeared in California. It is a remarkable character study of an ex-convict who has spent 15 years of unbelievable hell in prison—for a crime he did not commit! When his innocence is finally discovered, his mind has been turned simple by his ordeal, and Morrow dwells on the agony and suspicion felt by a man who has known nothing but inhumanity, as he attempts to adjust to *kindness*, thereby creating a unique type of horror.

"A Glimpse of the Unusual" in the April, 1880 issue of *The Californian* was a bizarre tale of psychological horror. A young newspaper reporter, before and after an ascent in a balloon, is asked "How do you feel?" The same question is put to him innumerable times on succeeding flights. Everywhere he goes during his waking hours, individuals approach him and ask "How do you feel?" When he threatens a man who is following him, the individual turns out to be a detective, who arrests him for his strange behavior. A committee is assembled to determine if he should be institutionalized. Believing that he is in danger of being committed for life to an insane asylum, as a result of some plot incomprehensible to him, the victim engages in a desperate duel of wits between himself and his examiners, aware that every answer he gives may be weighting the scales against him. Repeatedly, he is maneuvered by the detective, who seems to be masterminding the situation, into providing answers that will lead to his commitment to an asylum. When it appears that nothing will avail to save him, he suddenly changes his story and explains that all of his actions, along with all of his statements, have been part of an assignment from his newspaper to produce an "insider's story" of what conditions an individual is subjected to in the process of being declared legally insane and sent to an asylum. His examiners recoil from him as from a poisonous reptile. As he strides out of building a free man, he says to the detective: "You are a fool!"

The detective responds with: "And you are the devil." The reader is left with the impression that a man who is actually insane has brilliantly outwitted the authorities!

With that issue Somers sold the magazine to Anton Roman, the printer of the magazine and a San Francisco book publisher. The other stars—Roberta Duncan Milne, Emma Frances Dawson, and Ambrose Bierce—did not appear again but Morrow stayed on, to become the fiction mainstay of the publication for the rest of its two-year life.

His most unusual contribution was a novel-length detective story that could easily have been a model for A. Conan Doyle's Sherlock Holmes stories. It began in the September, 1880 issue and ran in seven installments through to March, 1881—about 60,000 words in length at a time when West Coast publications rarely ran novel-size serials. The title was *Strange Confession*. The locale of the novel is San José (where Morrow had secured a position as a reporter on the *San José Mercury*).

A shot is heard by a man and wife, who report it to the police. Barely has investigation begun when a youth walks into the police station and gives himself up as a murderer. On St. James Street, a young girl has died—of a small calibre bullet wound to her heart. Witnesses of the event are the confessor's mother and teen-age niece.

The 'detective' in the case is Chief of Police Casserly, who scents something unusual and elects to investigate the matter himself. He has had some success in difficult cases previously and for advice he always seeks out, as he does now, an 80-year-old judge of the Jewish faith named Simon. The old judge interprets behavior of individuals as well as the clues of a case. Suspicion, like the bouncing ball in silent movie sing-alongs, rebounds from the confessor to his mother, and then to his niece. An integral part of the story is the coroner, Garrett, who by means of an autopsy and scientific analysis accumulates considerable circumstantial evidence. At one point Simon, aided by Garrett, is following a lead to prove that the mother is innocent. Just when it seems that progress is being made, both the mother and the niece come forward, each claiming that *she* committed the murder. The investigators finally clear all three, when their evidence shows that none of them could have done it. But each had thought that one of the others had committed the crime, and had decided to save that one by confessing to the deed. Actually, the girl had committed suicide!

The plot may not seem so novel today, but in 1881 it was highly original and clever. The characterization was outstanding and the twists and turns the plot took were as modern as anything currently being written. Having been published in a regional magazine with limited circulation, the work never received the hard-cover publication it richly deserved.

Morrow's shorter works during the remainder of *The Californian*'s existence revealed a previously unexposed weakness. The man was no good at love interest, which apparently the new editor, Charles Henry Phelps, a practicing lawyer when he wasn't editing, insisted upon. "Rags, Sacks and Bottles" (August, 1880), in which two men duel to the death in costume at a Mobile Mardi Gras, was ruined by the injection of love interest, as was "The Music Teacher's Sweetheart," which appeared in the December, 1882 issue, *The Californian*'s last. Both, if written as straight horror stories, were baroque enough in images to have been successful.

This weakness was not present in "A Night with Death" in *The Argonaut* for February 5, 1881. It is a tale of a man who keeps vigil by the bedside of a dying friend, feeling he can frustrate the Grim Spectre by the sheer power of his will alone. To endure the agony he writes of another such vigil when another friend of his, Tom Burkett, was caught in the blast of steam from an exploding locomotive. Morrow's description almost makes the reader turn away as Burkett's eyes are blinded white, the skin peels away from his hands, and, as the injured man is gently guided away from the accident, bones and ligaments are plainly revealed. At first the shock and then the anesthesia dull his pain, but Morrow moves into a description of the all-but-inexpressible agony of the victim as the awakening nerves once again transmit their messages to the brain. Death defeats the will of the watcher once again, as it had done in the past.

Morrow's prominence in *The Argonaut* and *The Californian* led to the publication of his first hard-cover book, a novel titled *Blood-Money,* by the San Francisco firm of T. J. Walker & Co., in 1882. It was based on the Mussel Slough Affair. In California there was a huge tract of desert land on which nothing grew. Pioneers came in and with their own muscle and sweat dug irrigation trenches, enduring almost unbearable heat, dust, poverty, hunger, and derision as "visionary fools and dreamers." The land became some of the richest and most productive in the world. At that point, the Southern Pacific Railroad moved in, buying up the mortgages and utilizing every technicality to foreclose on the homes and parcels not yet paid for. They arranged things so banks would not extend further credit when there was a bad season, evicting those who were late in their payments without mercy or extension of time. With such methods, the railroad owners gained possession of the land and reaped an enormous profit.

This was the work that Ambrose Bierce later praised almost unreservedly in his "Prattle" column in *The San Francisco Examiner,* April 1, 1888. As part of the plot of *Blood-Money,* a leading character, Henry Webster, with the acquiesence of his brother, kills their father so that they can split the money they have taken from him. The money was buried under a tree for a time. Neither wishes to be the first to dig it up, and at one point Henry pays another man to kill his brother, so that he may have all the money. It is in this plot context that a dramatic episode of self-surgery (amputation of a leg) occurs, with the only instrument available being a pocket knife.

Bierce's accolade came far too late to do Morrow any good, and in the year 1882, it was widely believed tht the Southern Pacific Railroad sent a monthly check in outright grant or in the form of advertising to magazines or newspapers that promoted its viewpoint. In some case, the intent of drawing businesses and settlers—as well as tourists—to California was a laudable one. Other motives, such as the intent of gaining special privileges and tax exemptions, were considerably less commendable. As a result of these practices, most California newspapers and magazines did not review Morrow's book at all. If they did, they gave it short shrift, as did *The Overland Monthly* for February, 1883. Their anonymous review consisted of the following: "Mr. Morrow's new novel, *Blood Money*, deals with the Mussel Slough Affair, and is a very bitter indictment of the railroad company. Regarded as a novel with a purpose, it overshoots its mark by making out a case too bad to win credence; from a literary point of view, it is not equal to the author's average."

It was ironical that with the January, 1883 issue, *The Overland Monthly*, dead many years, had taken over *The Californian* and had been resurrected under the directorship of Millicent Washburn Shinn, a University of California graduate. She turned it into a completely bland publication, puffing various California industries. She also favored material written by women, often ninety per cent of the content of an issue being the work of women, some prefacing their last name with initials. It was said, with considerable justice, that her partiality towards women contributors was strongly influenced by the fact that she paid most of them nothing at all!

Not only was the magazine's editor hostile to Morrow; she probably would not have wanted such shockingly horrifying material in her pages at all. *The Argonaut,* while it did pay and paid promptly, did not pay well. His book having sold poorly, Morrow found himself in a very discouraging position.

Added to that were the increased responsibilities from his marriage to Lydia E. Houghton in San José on October 5, 1881. Lydia was 26 and a native of Iowa. Ten years later, in a brief biographical sketch of Morrow published in *The Story of the Files* by Ella Sterling Cummings, she wrote: "His wife, who is his chief critic and assistant...is herself gifted and able to write a first class story." No fiction of hers has yet been uncovered. In 1889 the City Directory of San José listed her occupation as telephone operator.

In 1881 and 1882 Morrow worked as a reporter on the *San José Mercury* and had taken up residence at "Lick House." At some undetermined period after their marriage the couple had a son who was either born dead or died shortly after birth. They never had any other children. There is evidence that during the first six months of 1881 Morrow resided in Fresno, California, a small city in the Sacramento Valley, one of the great farming areas of California. This is a logical deduction based on a unique policy *The Argonaut* then had. At the end of a story, they would place the city of residence of the author and the date the story was accepted. At the end of "A Night with Death" they appended Fresno and the acceptance date as February 1, 1881. Morrow, as yet unmarried, may have obtained a short-lived reporter's job on some newspaper in that community. When the last work he would write for *The Argonaut* for the next six years, "The Three Friends," was published in May, 1881, he was still in Fresno, and the date of acceptance was given merely as May, 1881. This was not fiction but an autobiographical item, recounting his life from the age of 13. He recalls that there were two oxen on the family farm near Evergreen, Alabama. He had no children to play with so these two oxen, named Buck and Brandy, were his inseparable companions. One day Brandy did not return from the fields with Buck. He was found lying on the ground, evidently dying from some poisonous vegetation he had eaten. The thirteen-year-old wrote a poem in blank verse to comfort the animal, and did not leave him until he died. The verse is reprinted in context of the account. The vignette ended with the words: "During the fourteen years that have passed since Brandy died, I have been in many strange places and have met many strange faces; but the memories that cluster around the death of Brandy, and those that linger about the loneliness of Buck, and his slow pining away and final death in spite of my constant care and solicitous friendship, are to me sacred recollections, and sometimes sad and bitter; yet more often sweet withal, and always tender." This was a revealing sentiment from an author who otherwise infused almost sickening horror into most of the fiction he wrote.

A check of the 1860 Agricultural Census of Conecuh County, Alabama, in which Evergreen was located, revealed that William C. Morrow, Sr. did indeed have a farm there. It consisted of 640 acres, of which 40 acres were improved; and he did have two oxen, so his son's vignette was unquestionably autobiographical. Evidently the farm was a sideline to the father's ministry, for in additon to the oxen there was one horse, one ass, three milch cows, nine other cattle, and 25 pigs. In 1859 the farm had produced 300 bushels of corn, 300 bushels of sweet potatoes, and 50 pounds of butter. Total value of the farm was $1,280 and total value of the livestock was $490.

The responsibilities of supporting a wife, coupled with the grinding disappointment of losing a good-paying market in *The Californian* and the failure of his first hardcover book *(Blood-Money)*, discouraged Morrow from continuing his writing of fiction. It should also be remembered that in those days a twelve-hour day was considered reasonable, so that a newspaper reporter went home when his managing editor told him he might. Besides, the five-day week had not yet been invented.

The couple took up residence at 214 N. Third Street in San José and in 1884 Morrow was temporarily out of the newspaper business and working as County Clerk at the San José Court House.

It was during the ten years following 1881 that Robert Duncan Milne became quite probably the most popular California author of the period, with a non-stop series of well-based science-fiction stories, most of them in *The Argonaut*. In his memoirs Jerome Hart, editor of *The Argonaut* following Bierce, had the following to say about Milne:

"Milne came of a good Scottish family. His father was a cleric of high standing. Milne was educated at the University of Edinburgh [actually at Oxford]. He had an unfortunate weakness for drink, which may have led his family to exile him to America. He received from them at intervals a modest remittance. During the short time this lasted he lived a prince and was surrounded by alcoholic courtiers. When the remittance was exhausted, he went to work writing stories.

And such stories! He possessed the power of making the possible seem possible. He took the *Argonaut* readers to the North Pole in an air ship. He led them into the bowels of the earth like a troglodyte. He flew with them into celestial regions with flying machines. He established communication with Mars by means of a colossal aerial reflector. He bombarded San Francisco with Chilean naval guns. He dropped dynamite all over California from hostile balloons. He hired buccaneers to steal seventy millions from the Federal Treasury in San Francisco. He brought to their notice a gentleman who remained frozen in a block of ice ten thousand years, but whom Milne kindly brought out and introduced. Finally, he destroyed the world in a terrific Cataclysm."

Milne was a sensation. His science fiction was reprinted in England and on the Continent and his science was absolutely ingenious. He would even give the proper manner to cast an airplane engine, which was extraordinary considering there would be no airplanes for another 25 years from the date that story appeared.

It undoubtedly was the example of Milne, whom Morrow had known and read since his earliest stories in *The Argonaut,* that broke his self-imposed writer's block. And so he wrote his first pure science-fiction story (though, being Morrow, it had to be science fiction of unrefined horror). Undoubtedly the fact that his old friend E. H. Clough had a story, "The Kiss of Death," about a man buried alive, in *The Argonaut* for September 1887 gave him further incentive.

Writing the type of fiction that Milne had made popular proved to be the right thing, for when his story "The Surgeon's Experiment" appeared in the October 15, 1887 issue of *The Argonaut,* the positive reaction and later reprinting—up to this day—exceeded that of his combined production previously.

A young man who has powerful reasons for wishing to die but is too cowardly to commit suicide pays a professor of medicine $5,000 to painlessly perform the act for him. Instead, the surgeon grasps this opportunity to conduct experiments in keeping a man's body alive with the head removed—not only alive, but growing and active.

A round metal ball is set in the center of the shoulders, and a silver tube descends to the stomach for feeding. Some instinctive ability seems to be retained by the motor nerves, which not only permit this unfortunate being to move about but to increase in muscularity and physical energy. One night the professor's wife hears strange sounds in the hallway and, walking in the dark, steps on a soft, floppy mass, which turns out to be this headless creature crawling about.

Her screams bring the surgeon running with a knife. He is unaware that the house has been quietly entered by detectives and police, on a tip—previously given them by the wife—that strange things were happening. They see the surgeon plunge a knife into a grotesque creature with a metal ball where its head should be. They watch him draw back to plunge the knife in the creature again. Powerful arms encircle the surgeon, and in the ensuing struggle an oil lamp is knocked over and a fire breaks out. The police flee the house and stand by helplessly as it and all its occupants are consumed in the flames.

Morrow had learned his lesson well from Milne. The scientific explanation of how such a headless creature could conceivably survive was long, excellent, and erudite. The virtue of Milne was that he never asked his reader to accept his extravagant speculations on faith, but offered elaborate, involuted, but clearly understandable and rational scientific arguments for his extrapolations. Certainly the secluded scientist conducting evil experiments was a stock literary device even in the 1880s, but it had been used successfully even by so distinguished an author as Nathaniel Hawthorne in "Rappacini's Daughter." Morrow sought to create a tale of horror based on "credible" foundations, and he succeeded.

William Randolph Hearst, Jr., was the son of a man whose worth was estimated at $20 million in 1887, possibly the richest man in California. The elder Hearst used this money to get himself elected to the Senate of the United States. In order to accomplish this, he had for some years run a newspaper, *The San Francisco Examiner*, the purpose of which was not really to make money, but to help Hearst get elected to office. He tried to get his son to take over the running of some of his gold and silver mines, but the boy had run off to New York and gotten experience working for Joseph Pulitzer on *The New York World*. To get his son to come back home and settle down, the elder Hearst offered him the *Examiner* to run for himself. It was turned over with the edition of March 4, 1887.

One of the first men Hearst Jr. hired was Henry D. Bigelow, who had been Ambrose Bierce's assistant on *The Argonaut* and had resigned shortly after Bierce left. Bigelow recommended that Hearst hire Bierce and he did, at $35 per week. Then Bigelow and Bierce urged Hearst to secure the writings of Robert Duncan Milne and of Morrow's friend E. H. Clough. With the publication of "The Surgeon's Experiment," they saw that Morrow was writing again, and writing at the top of his form. Within days of the appearance of his story in *The Argonaut*, the *Examiner* ran Morrow's "The Gloomy Shadow" in its October 16, 1887 issue. Morrow was then working as secretary of the Herald Publishing Company, the publisher of *The San José Herald*, and by 1889 he would become its editor. But Hearst paid extremely well by the standards of the day for outside fiction and articles he published, so Morrow's arm did not need to be twisted too hard.

In the 19th century the study of phrenology, a "science" which purported to tell an individual's character by the shape and bumps of the skull, was regarded as credible by many. In "The Gloomy Shadow" a professional phrenologist guides his childen's lives, directing them quite successfully into ventures and occupations at which they succeed. All except one boy who, confronting his father about his lack of guidance, finds the older man trembling with apparent fright, while uttering foolish words of praise but avoiding any advice as to a profession. The boy then consults another phrenologist who, after examining him, begin to shake with terror. After great pressure the phrenologist declares: "There is only one thing in life you are fitted to be, and it pains me infinitely to add that it is the only thing which Nature in her inscrutable wisdom has decided you cannot avoid being."

"And what is that?"

"A Murderer."

Though showing some evidence of being written hurriedly on demand, the story had every trademark of a typical Morrow horror story, finding frightening situations in seeminly ordinary events of life, in this case from a choice of occupations. If written today, a computer would have been substituted for the phrenologist.

Morrow's next story for *The Examiner* ran January 15, 1888 and was titled "The Jailor's Wife." While attempting to arrest a man for stealing a horse, a sheriff's son is shot and and killed. The horse thief is caught, convicted of murder, and is sentenced to be hanged. The killer asks the sheriff's wife, the mother of the boy he shot, to write a last letter for him. Upon hearing the information to be written in the letter, the sheriff's wife becomes almost physically ill and begins to behave erratically. The sheriff awakes one night to find his wife gone and the keys to the jail missing. Through the window, he sees his wife and the prisoner saddling horses. He fires at the prisoner but his wife throws herself in front of him, taking the bullet herself while the prisoner escapes. In a note she has left, the sheriff learns that the prisoner was his wife's brother!

Morrow strove for the ironic, and in his hands it became a successful device for trick endings that extracted maximum horror from seemingly conventional story situations. Had he also employed the sardonic, he could have qualified as a precursor of John Collier and Roald Dahl.

As it was, Ambrose Bierce, who had been conducting philological duels with Morrow in the pages of *The Examiner*, had published (March 11, 1888) "One of the Missing," the first of the stories, all in the style of Morrow, that would make him famous. During the Civil War, a scout on an observation patrol for General Sherman decides to take a shot at the Confederates before he returns with his report. As he cocks his rifle, his position is struck by a random shell. He finds himself buried in the debris, with the barrel of his rifle twisted to point straight at his head. Any movement may set off the hair trigger of the weapon! He sees hungry rats moving about, waiting for their opportunity. After a long period of pyramiding horror, he inches a board toward the trigger guard of the rifle and thrusts it upward. As he does so, his fear of imminent death is so overwhelming that he dies of fright. Unknown to the trapped man, the rifle had been discharged as it was jarred by the exploding shell.

Prior to this, the best of the few stories Bierce had written was "An Inhabitant of Carcosa," which appeared in the December 25, 1886 issue of *The San Francisco News Letter*. The style of this story, written in biblical prose, is nothing like Bierce's writing in "One of the Missing," nor would this new type of story be frequent for another year or so, not until Bierce had gotten the Swiftian mode out of his system with his novelettes of the future and dystopias as typified by "The Fall of the Republic, An Article from a 'Court Journal' of the Thirty-First Century," (March 25, 1888); "The Kingdom of Tortirra" subtitled "Some Account of the People of a Recently Discovered Country (April 22, 1888); and "The Tamtonians, Some Account of Politics in the Uncanny Islands" (November 11, 1888).

The first truly national literary attention both W. C. Morrow and Ambrose Bierce received was attributable to Fred Somers, who had employed Bierce as editor of *The Argonaut* and had approved purchase of Morrow's first dozen stories, including those he solicited for *The Californian*. Somers had made a killing on the stock market in New York City and with this money in his account, with the issue of July, 1888, he produced what Frank Luther Mott, in his fourth volume of *A History of American Magazines* described, with total accuracy, as "by far the most attractive and entertaining eclectic journal ever published in the English Language" in the form of *Current Literature*. When one realizes that Mott had examined every important magazine issued in America from the beginning to about 1920, it must be conceded that his endorsement was no idle encomium.

Current Literature was unquestionably the best literary review ever to appear in this country when Somers edited it. In its pages could be found discussions of popular culture as well as the classics, rediscovery of fine works that had been forgotten, news of the literary world from dime novel writers to Henry James, all handsomely printed and eminently readable. In his first issue, almost as if by design, Somers printed Morrow's second story from *The Argonaut*,"Awful Shadows," and Ambrose Bierce's recently published *Examiner* tale in the Morrow style,"One of the Missing." *Current Literature* rarely reprinted fewer than two works of fantasy and science fiction per issue while it was owned by Somers. Somers would also create the magazine *Short Stories* with the April, 1890 issue; this magazine would have an outstanding run through to 1962!

Practically the only review of any length ever written about Morrow previously was "The Art of W. C. Morrow" by Vincent Starrett in his book *Buried Caesars*. He begins the short essay with a rave about "The Permanent Stiletto," the book title for "A Peculiar Case of Surgery," which appeared in *The Argonaut* for February 4, 1889. Describing the opening of the story, Starrett wrote:

"There is more than a flavor of Poe in the lines; they are almost perfectly in the Poe spirit; Poe in the half whimsical, half sinister mood of The Cask of Amontillado. But Poe did not write them; they are the first two sentences in a story contributed years ago to a California journal by William Chambers Morrow."

Then, ironically, he suggests that Ambrose Bierce and Guy de Maupassant may have been other major influences on Morrow.

In "The Permanent Stiletto" a friend is found on a bed in a hotel room, with the handle of a dagger protruding from his chest. A surgeon called in for consultation says the handle belongs to a stiletto, which has penetrated the aorta. If the stiletto is removed, the man will die in minutes. The handle is severed, skin sewed over it, and the man is given anti-coagulants to prevent a blood clot and chemicals that might gradually dissolve the metal. A woman has

150

stabbed him because he refused to marry her. When the victim meets her again after five years, the traumatic shock is so great that he feels that the point of the stiletto has slipped from his aorta and that he is bleeding to death. When an autopsy is done, it is discovered that the muturic acid he had taken daily had gradually dissolved the blade and the tissues had healed.

Gertrude Atherton, renowned author and a strong supporter of Morrow, said she had never read a more dramatic opening to any story.

Following "A Peculiar Case of Surgery," Morrow had published what is probably his finest short story and unquestionably one of the great horror stories of all time. It was initially printed under the title of "The Rajah's Nemesis" but it is better known, even today, to thousands under the title of "His Unconquerable Enemy." It first appeared in the March 11, 1889 isssue of *The Argonaut*. The narration is made by a surgeon who is frequently employed by an Indian Rajah. He wins the Rajah's confidence when he successfully performs difficult surgery on a woman of the house.

There he meets Neranya, a male servant of the Rajah who bears great love and loyalty towards him but is possessed of a violent temper. This quality causes him to stab a dwarf to death one night; in punishment, the Rajah orders one of his arms to be cut off. His love for the Rajah now turns to hate, and he makes an attempt to kill him but is thwarted. The Rajah then orders the other arm cut off. Despite the loss of his arms, Neranya achieves great facility with his feet so that he can use them as arms. One night he kills one of the Rajah's sons and cuts both his arms off. The Rajah then orders both of Neranya's legs cut off, and he is suspended in a cage near the dome of the great Grand Hall and members of the staff ascend on ladders to feed him.

The Grand Hall is the coolest place in the palace on hot nights, so the Rajah frequently sleeps there in preference to his luxurious but uncomfortably warm bedroom. One night the Rajah's surgeon watches unobserved as Neranya, with his teeth, cleverly tears his clothing into strips, ties them together with the same technique, and by a supreme effort, for which he seems to have trained himself, lowers himself to the floor of the chamber. He does not head for the sleeping Rajah, but with arching, snakelike movements, drags himself over to a balustrade that curves up to a balcony.

With a mighty heave Neranya pulls himself up to the balcony and then drops twenty feet onto the sleeping form of the Rajah, crushing his chest and a moment later tearing out his throat with his teeth. The surgeon concludes: "His back had been broken in the fall. He smiled sweetly into my face, and a triumphant look of accomplished revenge sat upon his face even in death."

The writing is superb. The details of Neranya's incredible exploit were carefully thought out and delineated, and the revenge was appropriately horrible.

Morrow followed this in *The Argonaut* for April 29, 1889 with "The Type-Writer Exposed," a clever scientific detective story, told in a day when typewriters were still a novelty, even for writers. In order to establish a breach of promise suit, some letters are brought to an expert to prove that they all came from the same typewriter. The main thrust of the story is to itemize the scores of points in a typewritten leter, even when unsigned, that could be attributed to a specific individual. The material was ingenious, though it might have been better presented.

An increasingly rare diversion from mystery and horror was Morrow's "A Suggestive Suggestion," where a 75-year-old millionaire asks for a court decision on whether a legal marriage to a vivacious 19-year-old would find him free and clear of a claims from a woman with whom he had conducted an affair for 30 years and with whom he had sired a number of illegitimate children. This was an attempt at humor, and readers tended to yawn.

Robert Duncan Milne, writing science fiction, was in 1889 probably the most popular literary figure in the magazines and newspapers of the West Coast. W. C. Morrow trailed behind him but now undoubtedly ranked second. Coming up fast was Ambrose Bierce, who was again turning out horror tales in the Morrow style, sometimes even setting them in the South.

Undoubtedly again influenced by Milne's popularity and remembering how well "The Surgeon's Experiment" had been received, Morrow once again turned to science fiction. "A Dangerous Idea" in *The San Francisco Examiner for July 28, 1889* was reminiscent of Milne's story "The Man Who Grew Young Ago," from *The Argonaut* of February 19, 1887. In Milne's story, reverse aging was accomplished by temporarily attaching three individuals so their blood supply was intermingled for a substantial period of time. Morrow's story was the first of a series of science-fiction tales built around the character of a Southern scientist, Dr. Entrefort. This story is unusual because it involved scientific experiment against the background of slavery, with all the authenticity that Morrow was definitely capable of bringing to it. Dr. Entrefort has previously succeeded in attaching lower species of animals and fowls so that they share a common bloodstream and nervous system. A male slave, York, comes to Dr. Entrefort for permission to marry.

Entrefort, knowing the man is mentally unstable, denies him, but makes a counter proposal. If he will agree to the experiment of being temporarily joined together with the woman of his choice, sharing a common bloodstream, he will free them from slavery and give them $30,000 in gold and four slaves of their own.

The operation is successful and for a short time they are happy. Then York begins to complain that the girl is increasingly experiencing periods of irrationality. Dr. Entrefort agrees to separate them; he instructs them in how to stop the post-operative bleeding. At one swift stroke he severs them apart, but is unable to halt the girl's bleeding. She dies, though she reverts to complete rationality at the end. York becomes totally insane, tries to kill Dr. Entrefort, and in the process ignores the procedures for stopping the loss of blood and bleeds to death.

During the time the story was written, blood transfusion was an experimental procedure and was not standard anywhere. Medical knowledge of blood itself was primitive in 1889: the RH factor was unknown and blood types only sketchily understood. Transfusions, when given, were accomplished with syringes and injections. We know the implausibility of Morrow's premise today, but in 1889 the story unquestionably had tragic inevitability and power.

The Argonaut for May 19, 1890 ran a fine adventure story by Morrow, "A Cry for Help." A group of New Englanders buy a brig and sail around the Cape, where a storm unmasts the ship and throws it up on an uncharted island. There they encounter natives who live in stone houses, possess swords for weapons, and appear to be highly advanced. The natives tell them that from time to time small boats from nearby islands come by, and they can place them aboard one at a time to be taken to the mainland. In the meantime they are well fed. After a number of the men are led away, not to return, one member of the party follows. He discovers the latest man "to be set ashore" being flailed to death, a unique scheme to tenderize him prior to being cooked and eaten. He snatches a sword from one of the natives, cuts his friend free, splits the native king's head open, and the two of them escape in a small boat. Their story, reporting that they are naked and without food and water in an open boat, is found in a bottle by a man on a California beach. This story was later deservedly included in Morrow's hardcover collection as "A Story Told by the Sea."

Similarly treated was "An Unusual Conclusion" (July 14, 1890), retitled "An Uncommon View of It" for the book. A successful San Francisco lawyer discovers that his wife has been having an affair with his best friend. He buys a gun, intending to kill his wife, his friend, and himself. But he rationalizes the thing: what would the three deaths accomplish? If she ran off with the friend, they might find happiness. With his own suicide, in what way would that happiness conceivably bother him? However, he believes that his suicide would probably blight their happiness. He writes a note to her, explaining that he has been slowly dying of an incurable disease and does not want to continue suffering, and that she should look to his good friend for support. He then writes a letter to his friend, urging him to take good care of his wife after he is gone. He draws up a new will, leaving them all his wealth jointly, provided they marry within two years. Then, bright and happy, he blows his brains out. This was the type of spin that Morrow liked to put on a story.

Back in *The San Francisco Examiner* for January 4, 1891, Morrow displayed an astonishing ability to convert a travelogue of a trek up Mount Shasta into a tale of horror. Every roadblock, weather change, incline, or barrage of insects is converted into a contest with the supernatural in "The Lair of the Llaos"—until a day of sightseeing becomes an epic battle with the forces of nature and mystery.

"In a Dark Room" in the February 15, 1891 *Examiner* finds Morrow with a potentially powerful subject, carelessly handled. A sheriff needs to conduct a handcuffed prisoner back to town, but decides to spend the night in the back room of a store before proceeding. He handcuffs an arm and leg of the prisoner to his own, and they lie down to sleep. The sheriff awakes in the middle of the night to find the prisoner, who has mentioned that he suffered from a heart condition, apparently dead. The sheriff has thrown his pants, with the key to the cuffs in the pocket, across the room so the prisoner could not get at it while the sheriff was sleeping. In the pitch darkness the sheriff, dragging the dead body along, searches desperately for his trousers. The terror of the experience mounts until, in a combination of physical exhaustion and superstitious fear, the sheriff collapses unconscious. After recovering the key and freeing himself, the prisoner concludes the story with the statement: "Poor fellow! It was mean to play such a trick upon him, but it had to be done."

The lead-in is too long. The central portion of thrashing around in the dark with the "dead" body attached is up to Morrow's best level, but the ending is unconvincing and the reader has not been given adequate basis for accepting the logic of it. The piece was evidently hastily done under the inspiration of Bierce's "The Watcher of the Dead" from *The Examiner* of December 29, 1899, more than a year earlier. In Bierce's story, a man who elects to spend the night with a dead man in a pitch-black room is frightened to death himself when the corpse apparently comes to life in the middle of the night.

Then occurred a real-life irony as incredible as the plots of some of Morrow's more bizarre stories. The author of *Blood-Money*, the book that was to rip the curtain away from the play of the nefarious South Pacific Railway, accepted a job in the public relations department of the Southern Pacific Railroad at 404 Ellis Street, San Francisco, leaving his editorial post in San José. The question can reasonably be raised: was this a sell-out of his principles? On the part of Southern Pacific, was this an adroit buy-out of a former critic?

In *The San Francisco Examiner* for November 1, 1891 Morrow began a new mystery series entitled "Possible Solutions." In this he took famous unsolved cases in the San Francisco area and provided his own fictional resolutions of them. The first was "The Mysterious Case of William High." This was the case of a dead body, lightly covered with sand and with its pockets emptied, discovered in a San Francisco park. Morrow gathers all the clues and solves the matter very neatly, in the manner of Sherlock Holmes.

The second story in the series, "An Underground Hunt for a Chinese Menace," was the case of Frank Dempsey, a white man who ran a saloon with a Chinese clientele and who was stabbed to death in 1885, his murderer never found. Utilizing a Chinese-speaking detective and employing an action-packed investigation, including invasion of opium dens, Morrow proves through his fine characterization, outstanding narrative clarity, and skill at suspense—to be a heavyweight writer playing with a lightweight subject.

Morrow again demonstrated in "Her Love and His Lucre," a love story in *The Oakland Daily Evening Tribune* for December 19, 1891 that he was inadequate at romance. A package with $23,000 is found in the home of a young man who is known to have been on the premises from which $25,000 has disappeared. He is released from jail when a wealthy young girl, who is in love with him, testifies that she placed the money in his apartment to rescue him from debt. They live happily ever after.

In "The Woman of the Inner Room" (*The Argonaut*, January 12, 1891) Morrow returned to the thing he did best in this story with a theme that borders on telepathy. A man is found wandering around the streets of San Francisco in utter confusion. When examined, he is discovered to have a hole in his head, made by either a bullet or some sharp object. In an attempt to determine the nature of the wound, the doctor has his daughter (Miss Osborne) insert her little finger into the wound. Instantly the man becomes coherent. When she removes her finger he slumps into a stupor; when she re-inserts it, he resumes communication. Because the wound is round, it is presumed to have been caused by a bullet.

The daughter subsequently visits her fiance, also a physician, and finds him acting strangely. She determines that he is hiding a woman in the inner room of his office. From her contact with the wounded man, she feels that this woman is the person who shot him. The police consult a neurologist, who explains that her finger, inserted in the wound, establishes contact with a severed nerve, so that a message can be transferred up her arm to her brain and then back again to the victim. Therefore, both can read each other's mind; that is why the girl knows that the woman is the murderer.

The young doctor agrees to open the door to his inner office, but prefaces the act with an explanation. The woman who shot the wounded man, he explains, suffers from masked epilepsy. Epileptics have no memory of what they are doing during a seizure, and they are frequently confused in their actions. When the woman learned of the young doctor's betrothal to Miss Osborne, an epileptic attack was triggered, and she set out to kill the girl. Coming upon this other man first, she shot him instead!

When the door to the inner room is opened, out walks a matronly woman, well over fifty years of age.

"Miss Osborne and gentlemen, I have the honor to make you acquainted with my mother," the hitherto reticent doctor says.

This story is at one and the same time a tale of science fiction and a detective story, and like most of Morrow's works, cleverly involuted with a shocker at the end.

"The Wrong Door" by Morrow (in *The Argonaut* for February 9, 1891) is another grotesque tale of psychological horror. A man finds himself in love with Alice, the wife of his best friend, Dr. Brownell. He decides to bare his passion to the doctor and seek his psychological aid. Entering the doctor's home and office, he opens a wrong door and goes plunging downward into darkness. Seeking a way out, he opens into a great room with dozens of seated figures around a large table, Dr. Brownell among them. When he reaches out for Dr. Brownell, the doctor's head rolls off. Apparently they are wax figures. Then he sees what he assumes is a wax figure of Alice, but she moves and he embraces her. At first she seems to welcome his advances but then, horrified by his disheveled clothes and blood-stained face, she deduces his designs on her. The next thing he knows, a knife has been slipped into his chest and he passes out.

When he comes to, he is in bed being attended to by his friends. There is no wound in his chest and the only thing that puzzles them is why he smashed the two waxen images of them.

This is a baroque, surrealistic nightmare, which does not completely succeed, mainly because the very short sequences of love interest are awkwardly handled.

Morrow's "The Red Strangler" (in *The Argonaut* for May 18, 1891) is a combination of science fiction and mystery. The city of Boston has a mysterious strangler who has choked to death a series of prominent citizens, each of them for some alleged immoral act. Lewis Holbrook, a detective involved in the case, makes a trip to San Francisco. Holbrook survives a train wreck, but arrives in Frisco with one arm heavily bandaged.

Shortly after, a San Francisco man is choked to death, even with a police guard on hand. The guard himself is injured and irrational about what happened. The Chief of Police deduces that Holbrook himself is the strangler and the injured arm a decoy. Accosting Holbrook in another attack, the police chief is almost killed. Up to this point the tale is a well-plotted detective story, smoothly written and with vivid action. This proves to be a subterfuge for a work of science fiction, as Holbrook proves to be a human mutation born with one arm like a boneless tentacle, 42 inches in length and possessed of prodigious strength and dexterity. He uses this "arm" to strangle his victims.

"Christopher and the Fairy" (*The Argonaut*, August 10, 1891) was a complete departure for Morrow. It is about an elephant named Christopher and a fragile girl nicknamed Fairy. It recounts the frantic actions of the elephant—when the girl is killed in a fall—smashing through houses and fatally injuring himself following the transport of the girl's body. They are buried together above San Francisco Bay, their restingplace marked by a single monument with the line "Christopher and the Fairy" engraved on it.

"The Ape and the Idiot" (*The Argonaut*, September 14, 1891) is of importance primarily because it became the title story of *The Ape The Idiot and Other People*, Morrow's 1897 collection from Lippincott. An ape, escaped from a San José circus, inadvertently frees a 19-year-old idiot from a home for the retarded. From the branches of a tree, the two witness a ritual Chinese funeral, in which a child is buried in a shallow grave and food and drink are left in a brick oven to tide the departed over into the next world.

When all have departed, the ape and the idiot descend to eat the food. Out of curiosity they scoop up the loose dirt and open the coffin, reviving the little girl. The next morning the police find the three of them asleep by the open grave. In the book the story was retitled "Little Wang Tai." The situation is bizarre, all the characters unusual, but it scarcely rated to be the title story of a collection that contains a number of horror masterpieces.

In "Some Queer Experiences" (*The Argonaut*, December 21, 1891) five separate supernatural experiences are adroitly told, with William Morrow himself as a participant. He claims these events happened in the Old South at different stages of his life. Should we believe him?

The first story, "The Angel on the Housetops," tells of a woman who murdered her own child, boiled it, and fed it to her husband for supper. An angel seated on the roof shouts that if she will leave the house, a bag of gold will be dropped at her feet. Instead, a bag of stones is dropped on her head, killing her. In a second story, a men enters Morrow's home and asks for his father, the minister. Unearthly voices seem to urge the man to flee. He turns and hurries away; as he does so a scaffolding falls on his head, killing him. It is discovered that he had murdered his wife and had come to Morrow's father for help. There is still blood on his hands.

In "The Gigantic Katydid" Morrow tells the legend of rabbits that turn into giant red horses and carry off children. Out playing with a slave-child, Morrow one day sees a katydid grow into a large red horse. He becomes delirious for days; when he recovers, he learns that the slave child has disappeared and has never been seen again.

In "An Extraordinary Duel" Morrow has now reached the age of 19 and is at college. A strange man appears, identical in appearance to a person his uncle once killed in a duel. The individual has brought two rapiers with him; he tosses one to Morrow and forces him to defend himself. Morrow proves to be by far the better duelist, running the man through again and again but he never falls! Finally the stranger's weapon pierces Morrow; he passes out and when he comes to there is a healed scar on his side. On his return home he finds that he has been missing for two months. In the final story, "My Invisible Partner," the fictional Morrow, at the age of 21, receives a note offering to finance him in publishing a newspaper. A welter of items, which he never wrote, mysteriously appear in the paper—insulting, satirizing, and humiliating various people. On checking the original copy, he finds that it is indeed in his own handwriting. Readers love the material and the paper is quite successful. Unable to continue in that vein, he publishes a notice saying he will buy the paper from the owner, whoever he is. The offer is accepted and, in turning over the money, he discovers that the owner is a woman, who makes a prodigious leap from a building, from a height that should have killed her, and bounds off. Two months later, without her "assistance" the paper expires.

Of special importance is the preface to this group of stories which, if true (and the odds are that many of the remarks are true, as was the story of the two oxen in "The Three Friends"), would be the best explanation yet uncovered of the morbid and horrifying cast that shaded most of Morrow's stories through his entire lifetime. Here is part of what he wrote: "But I do wish to say (and these are facts with which many are familiar) that I was a sickly, nervous child from infancy; that having been reared in the South, my earlist mental development was largely the work of intelligent but highly superstitious Negro women—slaves—serving as nurses and housekeepers; that they filled my keenly sensitive mind with the most dreadful stories of ghosts, witches, devils, and the like, so that my childhood was passed in terror, my youth in morbid fancies, and my manhood, down to the present time, under the control of a gloomy and almost unmanageable imagination.

159

"In my boyhood, the most terrifying dreams would disturb my sleep; from these, I would often wake with paroxysms of screaming that my parents could not check in an hour. Somnambulism was a common experience, leading me into perilous situations, and giving concern to those charged with my safety. The slightest fever would inevitably send me into delirium, when the most grotesque and horrifying hallucinations—which would require a book to describe in detail—would haunt me.

"From all this, it may be judged that my temperament is abnormal, and that perhaps I have nervous peculiarities not common to the race."

This seems to coincide with the statement made by Will Clemens, editor of *Library and Studio*, concerning Morrow: "In years gone by Morrow was so thin it was necessary to look a second time," thus indicating that when Morrow arrived in California, he was not in robust health. His description of his early fragile nervous system seems to carry an air of truth and helps to explain what would otherwise be inexplicable.

In 1891 a weekly, illustrated competitor to *The Argonaut* titled *The Wave*, which had been started in Monterey in 1888 by J. O'Hara Cosgrave and Huge Hume, decided to shift operations to San Francisco. It ran news of literature, drama, criticism, humor, science, verse, local politics, and particularly outstanding fiction, eventually publishing a score or more of Frank Morrow's early short stories. While *The Argonaut* tended to appeal more to men than to women (despite its society page) *The Wave* had a distinctly feminine slant in much of its material.

Therefore it is not surprising that Morrow's first story for *The Wave* complied with this policy. It was redeemed from his customary failure on romantic themes by several factors. First, it further strengthened the fact of his closeness with Ambrose Bierce by making Bierce as well as himself the lead characters in the story, which appeared in the issue for March 7, 1891, and was titled "A Strange Adventure." Secondly, it gently spoofed Ambrose Bierce and the stories that had been circulating at the time about his appeal to women. Bierce had contributed two stories to *The Wave*, both with strong romantic interest. One of them, "The Widower Turmore," (January 10, 1891) was included in the first edition of *Can Such Things Be?* (1893) but was dropped from all future printings of that book. The second, "Haita the Shepherd," written in a style identical to that of "An Inhabitant of Carcosa," appeared in the January 24, 1891 number.

In "A Strange Adventure" Morrow and Bierce have taken a steam-driven cable car to The Cliff House (built in 1863 and destroyed by fire in 1894). Two women, a mother and her beautiful daughter, are overheard conversing in a deadly critical fashion about the two men. Despite this, Morrow can tell by the daughter's body language that she wants to meet him, particularly when she sends her mother home and remains seated. Morrow gets Bierce to leave and then approaches the young woman, who gushes all over him, compliments him on "the terrible stories you write, that keep me awake," and then adds, "I have worshipped you so long." The surprise ending comes when she concludes: "The supreme happiness of my life has come, and I could lie down now and die content; for have I not at last taken Ambrose Bierce to my heart."

Morrow resumed his series of fictionalized solutions to famous unsolved crimes with "The Tragedy of Lone Mountain" (*The Examiner*, January 24, 1892). This is the mountain with a giant cross erected on it by The Society of Jesus. In 1862 a mother and daughter were murdered in their home there, and the handyman was found buried about 150 yards from the house. Despite some datedly sentimental passages, Morrow's ability to evoke horror and dread rises to the standard expected of him.

"The Story of the Little Frog Catcher" was another in the series of fictional endings to unsolved mysteries (*The Examiner*, March 27, 1892). There had been a woman named Jenny Bonnet in the San Francisco area who dressed in men's clothing, hunted frogs, and sold their legs for a living. She spent her earnings helping prostitutes to start a new life, thus making their pimps her sworn enemies. She was killed by a shotgun blast while undressing for bed in a hotel room. The story is very skilfully written up to the point where Bonnet is shot. The solution turns on a man Jenny is about to kill because he had seduced Jenny's twin sister. She spares his life, but he is ungrateful to the point of paying a prostitute to be "saved" by Jenny, if she will act as the Judas Goat to maneuver Jenny to the window so she can be shot. Two men have been blackmailing him but when one of them realizes that Jenny has been killed, he utters a line that almost saves a sagging story: "God!" he cried, clutching the money, "this is the last cent I shall ever get!"

As a "regular" for *The Examiner*, Morrow was asked to write a contest story. It was to be titled "The Unfinished Story," beginning in the issue of June 12, 1892. The protagonist, Alfred Hamilton, after one year of marriage moves to a a cottage on the outskirts of town. The house is comfortable enough but has no entry directly from the house into the cellar. Hamilton conducts laboratory experiments of an unknown nature and undergoes personality changes. One day there is an explosion in the laboratory and he vanishes completely. The reader who would complete the story most satisfactorily would receive $50, with the second-place winner to get $25.

The winner was Joseph T. Goodman, former publisher of the *Virginia City Territorial Enterprise* (which had published some of Mark Twain's earliest works). Goodman's ending: It is discovered that there is a secret tunnel from the basement to a nearby building. The wife has found that the "changes" in personality of her husband are actually due to the substitution of his twin brother; she has become disgusted with this deceit. When the brother is arrested on a charge of safecracking, the police end up with both the men in custody because they are unable to tell them apart. The wife, sizing up the situation, identifies the twin (the safecracker) as her husband and walks him out to freedom, leaving her real husband to face the charges.

The second-prize winner, identified as Oliver T. Maklin, tells of the experiment that makes it possible for a man to alter his physical strength and personality. This explains his confusing personality changes. Goodman's ending is more like Morrow; it appeared in the July 10, 1892 *Examiner*.

One of Morrow's superior stories was "The Sunset Gun," which became better known after appearing in his collection as "The Faithful Amulet." It was published initially in the October 9, 1892 *Examiner*. A Malay steals an amulet that is of great price because it is reputed to bring personal safety and good fortune to the person who wears it. To the Malay's superstitious mind, this gives him freedom to murder and rob at will, with no fear of capture or reprisal. But he finds it does not prevent police and enraged citizens from pursuing him with a fury that results in his being shot and wounded. As he attempts to escape across the bay, his boat is destroyed but no body is found and the search for him continues. That evening, as usual, a blank charge is fired from a large gun at the nearby Fort. But, on this occasion, a spray of homogenized flesh, clothes, and bones falls upon a ship in the bay, on which the narrator is standing. There is a tinkle on the deck.

He bends and picks up a piece of metal. It is the stolen amulet. The Malay had hidden in the giant cannon!

Though everything that Morrow wrote was readable, not all of it was good. "By a Woman's Hand" (*The Examiner*, November 27, 1982) dealt with the famed Kearney riots of 1877, when unemployment in San Francisco sparked attacks upon the homes of the wealthy and on the Chinese. A woman who is a master of disguise plants a bomb in a carriage, intending to kill a newspaperman, who inadvertently avoids the trap. The story reads a bit disconnectedly, like a motion picture that has been edited so heavily that it no longer makes sense. It is impossible to tell whether historical events are being narrated or whether a supernatural element is being introduced.

Morrow's ability to create greater-than-supernatural horror from an understandable situation was exhibited in his model short story "A Tragedy on the Ranch" (*The Argonaut*, May 23, 1892). It is better known as "The Treacherous Velasco" in his hard-cover collection. A rancher back from a profitable sale of cattle gives his wife a small bag of gold. A ranch worker, Velasco, climbs into her window with a knife, but finds himself facing a gun in her hand. As punishment, he is stripped to the waist and tied onto a bucking bronco. The horse, frightened, goes kicking and rearing among a group of bee hives. The angry bees descend upon the hapless Velasco by the thousands as the horse kicks over more and more hives. By the time the horse is quieted and Velasco cut down, he has received the ultimate punishment.

In later years, Morrow would earn his living by teaching the proper construction of the short story. In tales like this one, he demonstrates that his qualifications for that occupation are impeccable. His ability to organize his material effectively and to render it without the use of a superfluous word is admirable.

For *The Argonaut* (September 5, 1892) Morrow turned in the second in his irregular series featuring Dr. Entrefort. It is in this story that we first learn that the scientist is a Creole, a Frenchman native to the United States.

During an operation Felice, the woman Entrefort loves, dies. He takes possession of the body for embalming and at the same time arranges to live with his widowed sister and her 18-year-old daughter. The daughter is difficult and disobedient; to correct this Dr. Entrefort plies her with a tonic that is helpful but seems to be habit-forming. She becomes cheerful and likeable. The girl's mother becomes suspicious of the change, and eventually learns that instead of embalming the body of Felice, Entrefort has reduced it to a chemical and incorporated it into the tonic he has been giving the daughter. Unknown to him, the formula contains elements of the disease that killed Felice, and now the daughter has become ill. This time the surgical skill of Entrefort saves his patient. He now wants to marry the young woman, claiming that his chemical has changed her into a completely different person. His sister dies from the shock of this development.

These early Dr. Entrefort stories are to a degree attempts to incorporate humor, which is not Morrow's forte. On another basis, set against the background of the pre-Civil War South, they actually represent a transition of the figure of the character of the "doctor" in science fiction from sorcerer to scientist.

"The Mated Rubies of Kyat Pyen" (*The Argonaut*, November 28, 1892) concerns two ruby rings, which draw the wearer of one to the wearer of the other, whosoever they may be. This is a Gothic tale, with great Scottish castles and elements of the supernatural, but despite excellent writing, the theme is too subtle and elusive for effective impact, something unusual for Morrow.

In September, 1892, *Lippincott's Monthly Magazine* published an All-California issue. As public relations man for the Southern Pacific Railroad, Morrow contributed an article titled "The Topography of California'" in which he covered the highlights of that great state. This may have been Morrow's first appearance in a nationally distributed magazine. Beyond that it helped establish a contact with Lippincott that would eventually result in the publication of his first book.

Contributing to *The Wave* for April 30, 1892, Morrow had made an interesting concession to that magazine's slant with his story "A Maiden Effort." Morrow alleges that the tale is written by one of his women students (apparently he was doing some instruction in writing as early as that). In the story, a girl has been given two gold garter buckles with diamond insets.

In one diamond she see the face of a strikingly handsome young man. In the other, the face of a fiercely staring "horrible" dwarf. She is told by a Hindu occultist that she must always wear the buckle in which she has seen the face of the handsome man on her left foot, otherwise she will experience something tragic. At one point, she mistakenly places the garters on the wrong feet. She faints as she is attacked by a giant dog. When she awakes in the home of a friend, the left garter is missing. There is a knock on the door and her eyes remain closed as the missing garter is placed in her hand and a soft voice speaks to her. She opens her eyes to confront the fearful dwarf she had seen in her garter buckle—and winds up in the insane asylum.

The real ending of the story is Morrow's epilogue, supposedly "correcting" erroneous details of his student's story, ending with the information that the garter buckle in question is now in his possession, and he will be pleased to return it if the owner will call for it. This was an attempt by Morrow to write a horror story in his usual line for a magazine that would have preferred something milder, by mitigating its impact in passing it off as a student's first effort.

The next story he did for *The Wave*, "The Queen of the Twelve Devils," (for their Christmas 1892 issue) was a marvelously written out-and-out fantasy for adults. A sufferer from asthma finds each attack preceded by a visit from a lovely girl, Sinovia, accompanied by a dozen utterly surrealistic "devils," each with a specific name: Pelim, whose blue whiskers grow from his nose and descend below his chest; Sargopee, with arms growing where his ears ought to be and a tail on the back of his head; Froup, a bright little fellow with four eyes; and all the others with decidedly unorthodox traits and nomenclature. They engage in antics absurd and menacing until Sinovia agrees to marry the sick man. He awakes from his latest asthma attack to find he has married Alice Fairweather, a girl who could have been a Sinovia clone. The fine writing makes this story worthy of preservation.

The previous year *The California Illustrated Magazine*, a publication serious in content and with outstanding format and printing, had appeared. Most of the contents of the first issue (October 1891) had been devoted to articles to promote various aspects of the state of California. Apart from the items of puffery was a short story by Morrow titled "The Removal Company," about a firm dedicated to helping people commit suicide and offering, as part of their service, disposal of the body. Investigation discloses that the company has used drugs to wipe out the memories of its clients, who are then sent out to unlikely locations to beg—for the profit of their "benefactors." Variations on this plot have frequently been used by other writers since Morrow (and probably by some before him).

Morrow continued writing for *The Examiner*. The January 8, 1893 issue featured his grim adventure story "In the Heart of the Mountain." The author and a young lady decide to make the 25-mile trek up Mount Shasta. Falling into a crevasse, they plunge into underground caverns in which they alternately almost freeze or are roasted, emerging just as the caverns are closing in on them. The situations are so well thought out and the writing so uniformly fine that the story ranks high despite the lack of a surprise ending.

By this time, were it not for the publication in 1891 of Ambrose Bierce's book *Tales of Soldiers and Civilians*, Morrow would undoubtedly have ranked as the leading literary figure on the West Coast. In "A Mystery of South Park," in the April 23, 1893 *Examiner*, Morrow once again produced an outstanding tale of horror. A woman appears in San Francisco claiming to be the survivor of a stint on a little-known Pacific island, from which she has brought back a hitherto unknown beast, which she plans to offer for sale. Concurrently there have been a series of mysterious deaths, in which the victims have been found crushed to death. The deaths are eventually linked to her when she is herself found dead, crushed by a gigantic python.

Particularly outstanding was Morrow's "A Mystery of the Fog" (*The Examiner*, May 28, 1893). A series of very young girls are kidnapped in San Francisco, later to be found wandering the streets, rendered speechless by an operation on their vocal chords. A young woman who has witnessed one of the kidnappings energizes her fiance, normally an extremely mild-mannered individual, to aid her in the search for this fiend. The shocker comes when she enters a room and finds her fiance in the process of operating on one of the little girls. He does not recognize her, and it is obvious that he is a completely split personality. He is a former surgeon, now with a passionate hatred for women because of an unhappy love affair, and therefore dedicated to rendering women speechless so that they will not injure another man. This narration of split personality is rendered with considerable power.

From time to time Morrow did columns of literary criticism for *The Examiner*, in which he displayed outstanding talent for this sometimes devastating art form. A whipping boy of his was "veritism," the form of writing that was the "essence of realism." Hamlin Garland annoyed him with his patronizing attitude toward California writers, who were admittedly ingenious in plotting and, in *The Argonaut* and *The Examiner* in particular, tended toward stories of science fiction, supernatural, and the off-trail. Linking Rudyard Kipling and Robert Louis Stevenson on the side of the "romantic" in fiction, Morrow presented his arguments on why they would be remembered long after the "veritism" of Hamlin Garland would be forgotten. He referred to Garland's tales as "refinement of the commonplace" and compared them to those "of the marvelous, of the terrifying, of the lofty and inspiring, the fanciful and the impossible, the fantastic, the capricious, the foreign, the whimsical, the unconventional, and the truly poetical." He charged many contemporary magazines with deliberately excluding such works. Ironically, Garland turned to spiritualism in his later years!

In that same issue of *The Examiner* (March 5, 1893) Morrow had a collaboration, "The Son of a Warrior," with Luella Green Harton, who may have supplied the legend upon which the story was based. It tells of a blind Indian boy who is regarded as useless, so when he is grown he is abandoned in the deep woods to die. He survives, gradually regains his sight and returns to save his tribe from defeat by its enemies, later leading them to prosperity. Once this is accomplished, he disappears and is never seen again. Morrow wrote this in the manner of an Indian legend, lending it a considerable grim beauty.

The "romance of the steam engine" was the subject of a series of four short pieces of Morrow's included under the collective title of "Stories of Locomotive Engineers." It was his point that there is an almost mystical bond between steam locomotives and their engineers. All of these stories are alleged to be "true." In "A Tragedy in the Marshes" a locomotive tries to kill its engineer for cursing at it. A suicide pact is carried out between an engineer and his locomotive in "The Story of a Double Suicide." In "The Victim of the Cloud Burst" he departs from his horror formula to sentiment—to tell how a tramp, permitted to ride in a train against company rules, saves a child from death. Morrow is nothing short of masterful in his construction and narration of all these stories, including the introductory tale of a ship's engineer who has learned to communicate with his steam engine.

Undoubtedly near the top of Morrow's production of unusual short stories is "Over an Absinthe Bottle," reprinted many times, even as a separate pamphlet by The Book Club of California in February, 1936. It appeared originally under the title of "The Pale Dice-Thrower" in the January 2, 1893 issue of *The Argonaut*. The changes from this earlier version to that of the book version and later reprintings were minor, a major one being the switching of the protagonist's name from Carringer in *The Argonaut* to Arthur Kimberline in later printings.

The protagonist is literally dying of hunger. He has eaten nothing in 70 hours. Everything he owns, except the skimpy clothing on his person, has long since been sold for food. The only choice that remains to him is whether he prefers to die of starvation, exposure, or suicide. As a refuge against the chilling rain, he is invited into a tavern for a drink by a man who possesses "a death-like pallor." The stranger takes him into Booth 7, peels out a roll of bills and purchases a bottle of absinthe and some water and locks the door. The stranger tells the protagonist he may keep the change to play him a game of dice for a dollar a game.

The man is dying of starvation, so the absinthe simply stimulates his hunger. The game's fortune sways back and forth; the stakes rise steadily until they have reached a thousand dollars a game. Though the protagonist's winning mount to $74,000, he suffers excruciating agony as hunger pangs consume him. Finally the stranger suggests one toss of the dice for the whole pot, and the stranger wins!

The protagonist must now leave, still on the point of dying of starvation, with $148,000 heaped on the table before his eyes. But then he observes that the stranger is reclining, with a strange whiteness on his face. He is dead! The money can all be his!

He arranges the money into neat piles. Stuffs some in his pocket. Exits. Now he is *enjoying* the hunger, knowing that he can appease it in any manner he wishes. To be hungry with money in one's pocket is heaven!

Several detectives burst into Booth 7. Two men are seated at the table with neatly arranged parcels of money and an empty bottle of absinthe between them. Both are dead!

Did the protagonist die of hunger immediately following his realization that his opponent was dead, and in his final moments imagine that he was stuffing money into his pockets and leaving the premises. Or is it a tale of the supernatural, where his spirit still possesses awareness and the ability to leave? Either way, it is an authentic American literary classic that deserves to be more frequently anthologized.

"My Partner at Whist" (*Argonaut*, September 4, 1893) is important because it represents a definite turn on Morrow's part away from the attitudes of the Confederacy and toward the Northern point of view. A Northern mathematician, after the Civil War, rents space in a Southern home in order to quietly carry out some very important astronomical calculations. The Ku Klux Klan, suspicious of his activities, is watching him intently. One night they raid the house and carry him off, along with a young woman living in the house. They throw the two of them into a mass of cotton and begin to compress the cotton into bales that will be loaded on a ship for England the next day. Morrow exploits the horror of the situation up to the point where Federal soldiers finally show up. Untypically, Morrow permits a happy ending as the mathematician marries his partner in the harrowing experience.

Far more grim was "The Unfaithful Clock" (*Argonaut*, October 16, 1893). This is a story of Austin Wheeler, whose wife has run off with another man. When a child resulted from the union, the illicit lover murdered her on that very day. Wheeler hounded the murderer to the gallows but was not satisfied. He has a wall clock constructed so that at eleven o'clock every night, at the striking of the hour, a hooded figure, an effigy of the individual who ruined his life, drops from a gallows. Ritualistically, he has watched the performance for thirty years.

But then the hooded figure begins to appear at midnight rather than at eleven o'clock. This continues, no matter what adjustments are made—an indication that something very unusual if not supernatural is occurring. The conclusion comes as the son of the murderer enters the room and chokes Wheeler to death. Instead of some surprise incident to end this powerful story, Morrow simply quotes this second murderer's words as he gazes at his severely lacerated hands: "Damn the brute! Who ever heard of a cat fighting for its master's life?"

By the end of 1893 Morrow had left the employ of the Southern Pacific Railroad and had taken a position as editor of *The San Francisco News Letter*. That publication was started by an Englishman, Fred Marriot, Sr., who had founded the famed *London Illustrated News* and had been the editor of the *London Morning Chronicle*. He appeared in San Francisco as early as 1856 and in July of that year launched his *News Letter*. He was an inventor and while still in England had patented a steam-driven lighter-than-air dirigible. In the United States he formed The Aerial Steam Navigation Company in 1866 and had established his patent as valid in 1869, selling stock in his company that year. On July 3, 1869 he flew successfully in the presence of hundreds of witnesses. He took photos, which still exist, of the flight of his experimental machine, which he called *The Avitor*. It was a non-rigid dirigible-shaped balloon filled with hydrogen, with wings to stabilize it and a steam boiler and steam engine suspended below to provide power. It was 37 feet long and 11 feet wide, with propulsion propellers on the wings. The ship was controlled from the ground by ropes fastened to the rudder and elevators. It rose from the ground and circled a race track twice at about five miles an hour. The performance was repeated in Mechanics' Pavilion in San Francisco. A ten-day trip to New York was planned, but someone carelessly lighted a match near the hydrogen and the marvelous machine blew up. No known attempt to reconstruct it was made.

But the *News Letter* survived. It was a weekly, with three columns of news on the front page and the other side blank, except for Midsummer and Christmas issues, which were enlarged and ran fiction. For a short period Ambrose Bierce was editor; by the '90s the older Marriott had died and his son was running the paper.

The Christmas 1893 number ran a short story by Morrow entitled "The Sheriff's Prisoner." It was one of his tales of irony. The sheriff of Hangtown is known to be bringing back, on a train, the vilest, most dangerous criminal in the West. He is greeted by a mob, who overpower him and in no uncertain terms, with a noose waving the air, demand that he turn the criminal over them. He meekly leads them to the baggage car, has the door opened, and there—on ice—is the dead carcass of the bandit!

Morrow's days as a "regular" in the literary columns of *The San Francisco Examiner* were just about at an end. San Francisco was bragging about a Midwinter Fair in 1894, and they had a page titled "Our Authors at the Fair" in the January 28, 1894 issue. In addition to Joaquin Miller, Henry D. Bigelow, R. A. Morphy, Frank M. Pixley, and Frank B. Millard, W. C. Morrow had a short piece titled "A New Group of Liars," which complained that since Californians had a reputation for superlatives, no one would believe how really good the Fair was. There were some artists' drawings of the Fair, but on reading all the accounts it was literally impossible to determine from them whether they were reporting on a fair that had been held—or drumming up business for one still to take place.

In the same edition Morrow had an impressive illustrated full-page feature titled "Our Marvels Above and Below Ground" which read like a holdover from his job at Southern Pacific. It extolled the marvels of the state of California, but its greatest appeal to fantasy lovers was its picturesque statement: "Let us picture the Gulf of California as we know it to have been ages before Queen Calafia unleashed her griffins and destroyed the pagan fleet which sought the destruction of Constantinople." This was a direct reference to the origin of the name of California, culled from the fantasy volume *Sergas of Esplandian* by Garcia Ordonez de Montalvo. This was first published in Spain in 1510; germaine sections of it were translated as "The Queen of California" by Edward Everett Hale in 1872 for delivery before the American Antiquarian Society in April of that year. It was included in his book *His Level Best* (1873) after prior publication in *The Atlantic Monthly*. Montalvo's book was the first to use the name "California" and told of a black race of Amazons who rode griffins into battle.

The first phase of Morrow's career, that phase in which just about all of the stories included in his book *The Ape The idiot & Other People* were written and published, can be said to have ended when the book's eventual publisher, Lippincott, ran his short story "The Inmate of the Dungeon" in the March, 1897 number of *Lippincott's Magazine*. A prisoner, known as Convict No. 14,208, is called in for review by the Chairman of the Board of State Prison Directors, despite the fact that the prisoner has made no request for such a review. The prisoner tells his story: he had been sentenced for killing a man who robbed him. Offered time off for good behavior, he had been a model prisoner. He often volunteered for extraordinarily hard physical work, and was rewarded with additional portions of items such as tobacco. One day he lined up for his portion of tobacco but was told he already had received it and was accused of trying to cheat and get more than he was entitled to. This set off a battle of wills between him and the warden and the prison guards that resulted in years in solitary, fed only on bread and water. He was whipped repeatedly, but he refused to go to work until he got his plug of tobacco. He threatened to kill the warden when released, and so he has been kept in solitary confinement for 23 consecutive months. At the end of the testimony a doctor examines the man and sends him to the hospital.

Three weeks later he is brought in, unmanacled, and left alone with the warden, with the door locked behind him. The warden informs him that a recently released prisoner has sent a letter confessing that he was the one who got the extra plug of tobacco. The warden admits that he has treated the prisoner with excessive cruelty, that if he had understood the true circumstances he would not have done so. Nevertheless, the warden had been forced to resign; but before doing so he arranged that the prisoner should be granted a pardon. As a result of this situation, both their lives have been ruined, and the warden realizes, he laments, that his conscience will punish him for the rest of his life. Rather than suffer it, he offers the former prisoner a gun to complete his revenge. "You have done it at last!" the man weeps. "You have broken my spirit. A human word has done what the dungeon and the whip could not do...I'll go...I'll go to work...tomorrow."

There is a similarity in theme between this story and the earlier "The Man From Georgia." Both proved very popular and the critics selected "The Inmate of the Dungeon" as the finest in the volume. It was a pioneering psychological study in fiction form and one can admire its organization. It was ideal for a stage play and was produced in 1925 by Holbrook Blinn in New York City as a one-act play.

In reviewing the content of this overview of the reputation-gathering phase of W. C. Morrow's career, it may seem that excessive praise has been heaped upon him. That is not true. Along with those stories covered and those yet to be covered in this, the first and only existing outline of William Chambers Morrow's writing career, (and in addition to the 14 stories contained in his collection *The Ape The Idiot & Other People*), at least another 30 stories deserve to be permanently preserved, some of them as great American short stories, with full recognition of the meaning of the word "great." To illustrate how ephemeral is literary fame and how easily it may be lost, it is probably accurate to say that the author of this present essay is the only man alive on the face of the planet who has ever seen and read most of W .C. Morrow's output. In some cases, the photocopies can never be duplicated because the original microfilm is already lost or is crumbling, and though kept in the dark, the negatives of the photocopies are gradually fading.

Key References Available on W. C. Morrow

Fiction

Morrow, W. C. *The Ape The Idiot & Other People*, Lippincott, 1987. A critical success and good seller, containing many very fine short stories.

Howard, Eric. "W. C. Morrow" on pages 187-188 in *California and the Californians*, edited by Rockwell Hunt, 1926. Contains numerous misstatments and errors of fact, but includes a number of items not available elsewhere.

Moskowitz, Sam. *Science Fiction in Old San Francisco: Volume I, The History of the Movement* (Donald Grant, 1980). More information on Morrow up to the year 1890 than is available from any other source; also the definitive depiction of the fantasy boom in San Francisco from 1850 to 1890.

Starrett, Vincent. *Buried Caesars*, Chapter 5, "The Art of W. C. Morrow" (pages 118-125). An appreciation of Morrow by the famed bookman, but wrongly suggests that Bierce was Morrow's major influence, when the reverse was true.

Contributors

Darrell Schweitzer is the author of nearly a hundred stories published in *Twilight Zone, Night Cry, Amazing,* and elsewhere, and of two fantasy novels, *The White Isle* and *The Shattered Goddess.* Some of his short fiction has been collected in *We Are All Legends* and Tom O'Bedlam's *Night Out.* He is also a reviewer, interviewer, essayist, editor (of the *Discovering* series for Starmont and of the revived *Weird Tales* magazine, and co-editor of the anthologies *Tales from the Spaceport Bar* and Another Round at the Spaceport Bar); writing instructor, and literary agent.

S.T. Joshi, inevitably referred to as "the indefatigable S.T. Joshi," is the leading Lovecraft scholar of the present day, the author of the Starmont volume on the Old Gent, compiler of *H.P. Lovecraft, An Annotated Bibliography,* and editor of *H.P. Lovecraft, Four Decades of Criticism* and two journals, *Lovecraft Studies* and *Studies in Weird Fiction.* He also has a major scholarly interest in Arthur Machen and Lord Dunsany. His supperlative *The Weird Tale* was a 1990 World Fantasy Award finalist.

Alan Warren is a freelance writer based in the San Francisco Bay area. He has published fiction since he was 18, in *Mike Shayne Mystery Magazine, Isaac Asimov's Science Fiction Magazine,* and elsewhere. He also writes film commentary and is working on a novel.

Lee Weinstein is the author of a small body of distinguished fiction and criticism, including the striking story "The Box" (in *Whispers II*) and articles on Charlotte Perkins Gilman and William Hope Hodgson.

Ben P. Indick continues his record of publishing in *all* of the Schweitzer-edited Starmont books. He is (obviously) an essayist of note and also a playwright, author of the critical study *The Drama of Ray Bradbury,* and publisher of the Lovecraftian fanzine *Ibid.* He is a member of the Esoteric Order of Dagon.

Gary William Crawford holds an M.A. in English from Mississippi State University. He was editor-publisher of the journal *Gothic* and now edits the Gothic Press Chapbook series. He has published essays on Le Fanu, Ramsey Campbell, Robert Aickman, Joyce Carol Oates, and Stephen King. His fiction has appeared in *Weirdbook, Fantasy Tales,* and *Dark Horizons,* among other places.

Mike Ashley is a leading British critic/anthologist/scholar who has helped produce many of the crucial reference works in the field, including *Monthly Terrors* and *Science Fiction, Fantasy, and Weird Fiction Magazines*. His writer-profiles have appeared in *Twilight Zone*. He has recently produced a bibliography of Algernon Blackwood.

Sam Moskowitz's accomplishments are almost too extensive to enumerate, ranging over the decades from *The Immortal Storm* (a history of science-fiction fandom in the 1930s) to managing editorship of Hugo Gernsback's *Science Fiction Plus* (1953) to much recent, pioneering research into 19th century SF and fantasy, which has resulted in the rediscovery of several writers. He has also edited *Reflections in the Moon Pool*, a volume of uncollected A. Merritt material, to which he contributed an introduction so extensive it amounts to a biography. He has done the same for William Hope Hodgson in *Out of the Storm*. He was one of the very first historians of science fiction; his *Seekers of Tomorrow* was among the first books *about* SF ever to achieve wide circulation. He has edited *Science Fiction by Gaslight, Under the Moons of Mars*, and numerous anthologies, and has also written a small amount of fiction. He is a recipient of the Pilgrim award for SF scholarship.

Index

187

Summers, Montague, 28
  The Supernatural Omnibus, 28
Swedenborg, Emmanuel, 95, 96, 97, 98
  Heaven and Hell, 98

The Temple Bar, 95
Thorns (Robert Silverberg), 73
"Three Lines of Old French" (A. Merritt(, 81
T.P.'s Weekly, 8
Twain, Mark, 162

Van Doren Stern, Philip, 1
Vanity Fair, 35
Victoria (Queen of Great Britain), 100, 103
Virginia City Territorial Enterprise, 162

Wakefield, H. Russell,m 73-91, 116
  "The Alley," 83
  "Animals in the Case," 89
  "Appointment with Fire," 90
  "Blind Man's Buff," 80
  The Clock Strikes Twelve, 82, 83
  "Damp Sheets," 80-81
  "Day-Dream in Macedon," 81
  "The Death of a Bumblebee," 90
  "Death of a Poacher," 82
  "Farewell to All Those," 85
  "Four Eyes," 86
  Gallimaufry, 80
  "Ghost Hunt," 86-87
  "The Gorge of the Churels," 87-88
  The Green Bicycle Case, 81
  Happily Ever After, 80
  "He Cometh and He Passeth By," 76-77
  Imagine a Man in a Box, 80
  "Immortal Bird," 89
  "Ingredient X," 84-85
  "Into the Outer Darkness," 83
  "Jaywalkers," 84
  "A Kink in Space-Time," 87
  "The Last Meeting of Two Old Friends," 89
  "Look Up There," 79-80
  "Lucky's Grove," 84
  "The Middle Drawer," 86
  "Not Quite Cricket," 82-83, 84

www.ingramcontent.com/pod-product-compliance
Lightning Source LLC
Chambersburg PA
CBHW020855090426
42736CB00008B/382